The Turret Clock Keeper's Handbook

(New Revised Edition)

Cover Picture: Turret Clock in St Ann's Church, Limehouse, by John Moore of Clerkenwell 1839.

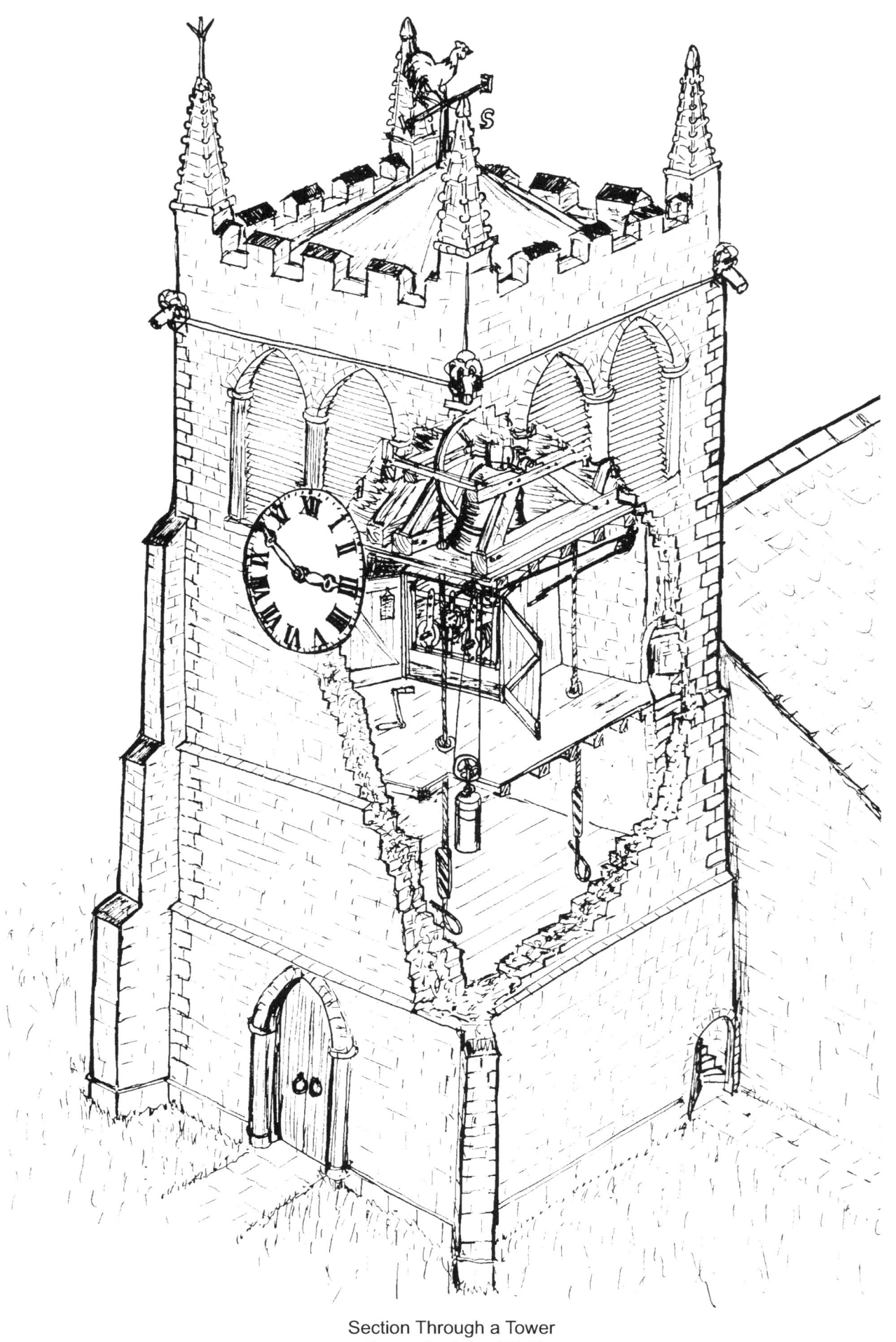

Section Through a Tower
Drawn by John Ablott

THE TURRET CLOCK KEEPER'S HANDBOOK

(New Revised Edition)

A Practical Guide
for those who
Look after a Turret Clock

Written and Illustrated

by

Chris McKay

Copyright © 2013 by Chris McKay
All rights reserved

Self-Published by the Author
Produced by CreateSpace
North Charleston SC USA
ISBN-13:978-1492317708
ISBN-10:1492317705

CONTENTS

Introduction 11

Acknowledgements 12

The Author 12

Turret clocks— A Brief History 12

A Typical Turret Clock Installation 14

How a Turret Clock Works 16

Looking After a Turret Clock 19
    Basic safety... a brief introduction 19
    Manual winding 19
    Winding groups 21
    Automatic winders 21
    Setting to time 21
    Setting summer time and winter time 22
    Regulation 23
    To start a clock should it have stopped 23
    Correcting the striking or quarter striking 24
    Night silencing 25
    Bell hammers 25
    Electrical clocks 25
    Expected timing performance 25
    Your Successor 25

Turret Clock Terminology 27
    Describing a turret clock 27
    Frames 27
    Electrical clocks 30
    Escapements 31
    Pendulums 33
    Weights, lines & pulleys 33
    Dials 34

Automatic Winders 35

Night Silencing 37

Automatic Correctors 38

Electro Hammers 39

Turret Clock Maintenance 40
    Basics 40
    Safety checks 40
    Cleaning 41
    Lubrication 41
    Record sheet 42
    Basic preventative measures 42
    What to do if a clock has stopped 42
    Basic diagnostics 43
    Dials and motionworks 43

Restoration and Conservation 44
    Terminology 44
    Statements of significance and need 45
    Statement of significance 45
    Statement of need 45
    Restoration and conservation policy 46
    Beyond economic repair 46
    Dials 46

Commissioning Turret Clock Work 48
    Deciding on the needs 48
    Requesting a quotation 48
    What a quotation should contain 49
    Reasonable exclusions 49
    Unreasonable exclusions 50
    Assessing a quotation 50
    Warranties 50
    Installing automatic winders 51
    Dials and motionworks 51
    Moving turret clocks 51
    Illuminating dials 52
    Adding quarter striking and tune playing 52

Who will do the Work Required? 53
    Finding and choosing a turret clock restorer 53
    The approach to the work required 53
    Qualifications 53

Other Issues 55
    Replacing a mechanical turret clock 55
    Retiring a mechanical turret clock 55
    Lifetime costs 56
    The future for retired clocks in Church of England buildings 56
    Weight chutes and pulleys 57
    Old electrical clocks 57
    Church of England faculties & DAC Advisers 57
    Publicity 57
    Fund Raising 58

Health & Safety 59
    Safety in visiting a clock for winding 59
    Locked in strategy 59
    Risk assessment check sheets 60
    Turret clock health & safety survey check sheet topics 61
    Mobile phone transmitters 63
    Mercury in turret clocks 63

Collecting Turret Clocks 65
    Collecting philosophy 65
    Points to consider 65
    Acquiring a clock & provenance 65
    Restoration 66
    Disposal 66

Turret Clock Recording 667
    Turret clock recording form 68

Glossary of Terms 70

Turret Clock Sources of Information 73

Bibliography 74

Instruction Sheet that can be Hung in a Clock Case 80

Turret clocks are so very diverse in their design and construction that it is highly unlikely that the illustrations, which are given in this booklet as a guide, will be exactly like the clock for which the keeper is responsible. However, it is hoped that they will convey the spirit of the text and help as much as possible. All pictures are based on real clocks and an indication of the period of the feature has been given where possible.

[9]

Introduction

The objective of this book is to give practical advice to those who look after a turret clock. The book was first published in 1998 by the Turret Clock Group of the Antiquarian Horological Society. Being passionately concerned with turret clocks in England, my aim in writing the book was to promote the preservation and conservation of these clocks through providing information on their proper care.

Over 4,500 copies have been printed, sold or given away. Some years later I put the book up on my web site as a free download. I have no idea how many people chose to download a copy but it must be several thousand.

In 2013 I decided to update the book since things had changed in two fields. The first is health and safety and the second new technical developments. New information has been integrated where possible into the original contents or added at the end. Some of this new information does not lend itself to the graphic treatment used in the original book so please excuse expanses of text.

I did not want to be distracted with printing, storage and distribution so I made the book available as print-on-demand through the internet. Over the years I have had many communications with people in North and South America, Europe, Africa, India, Australia and New Zealand. My chosen means of production meant that anyone in the world can have easy access to this book.

There are many mentions about church clocks in the book; the reason is simple, there are so many church clocks in England. Comments on church clocks can generally be equally applied to any other turret clock.

I have used Imperial measurements since those were the ones in use when the clocks were made.

Disclaimer: All the information and guidance in the book has been given in good faith. I accept no responsibility whatsoever for what you do and the consequences you might create. The situation of each turret clock is unique so please check with all people involved with the clock before taking any actions and do involve a professional turret clock restorer. However, I do hope that what I have presented here is useful and will help turret clocks to be enjoyed by future generations.

Chris McKay

Dorset England
September 2013
chris.mckay@tesco.net

Acknowledgements

Many people read through the various drafts of this booklet and offered helpful alterations, additions and corrections. To all those who assisted me I offer my thanks, without them The Turret Clock Keeper's Handbook would have been a very incomplete book. I would like to thank especially John Ablott, Jonathan Betts, Derek Frampton, David Knight, Chris Pickford, Mike Trickett, Keith Scobie-Youngs, Geoff Sykes and Peter Watkinson, who all made valuable suggestions.

The Author

Chris McKay's interest in turret clocks started when he was 11. His first restoration job began when he was 18 and took 10 years. Since that start he has seen many hundreds of turret clocks and taken thousands of photographs. An early member of the AHS Turret Clock Group, Chris was much affected by the enthusiasm of the late David Nettell. He is a Chartered Engineer who has a broad experience in the electronics industry from field service through to sales and marketing. After a career move, he went into teaching technology and computing in secondary schools and finished his career in a leading prep school.

Turret Clocks— A Brief History

What is a turret clock? It is a clock which is intended to make the time known publicly either by striking on a bell or bells, showing the time on an external exposed dial, or both.

No one knows who invented the first clock, or where, or when. However there are some things we do know; one of these is that during a night in 1198 there was a fire in the Abbey church of St. Edmundsbury. Monks put the fire out using their cowls, water from the well and water from the clock; so the Abbey had a water clock!

It is thought that mechanical clocks, as we would recognise them, first made their appearance about 1275 on the continent. We have very little information about these clocks, a common speculation is that they hung on a wall and had an alarm to wake a monk who would then go and ring a bell in the tower to summon his brothers. A large clock had enough power to strike a bell in a tower… and thus the turret clock was born.

Turret clocks spread throughout churches, monasteries, royal palaces and all places where there was a large number of people working together. When country houses were built, turret clocks were almost always put up, usually over the stable block. Here they would have kept time for the whole estate, regulating the life of all from the youngest stable lad to the Lord of the Manor himself.

Army and Navy barracks too had turret clocks. When factories started to be set up during the early 19th century turret clocks again appeared on these buildings to summon the workers, and to dismiss them at the end of the day. In the village, like the town, the church clock regulated the affairs of people meeting together.

Turret clocks were set from a sundial, which meant that clocks in towns across the country did not tell the same time due to their different longitudes. Differences across the UK could be up to 30 minutes, but this was quite adequate for local use since no one could travel fast enough to notice. In the 1830s when trains started to run across the country; a common railway time was agreed in the 1840s leading to Greenwich Mean Time being adopted as the National standard in 1880.

It was not until early in the 20th century that the turret clock declined in importance. Thanks to imports of cheap pocket watches from America and Switzerland, many people started to use their own timepiece. Wrist watches appeared on the scene around the 1890s, and were in common use at the time of the First World War, so their greater convenience led to an even further decline in the need for public clocks.

Today time is easily available to us all. Radio broadcasts time signals and almost every appliance has its own built-in clock. The speaking clock on the telephone gives precise time, mobile phones all have clocks and the amazing accuracy of quartz watches along with their low cost, really means that the turret clock is no longer needed in the way it was when it was first installed. However, those who care for a turret clock will well know just how highly it is regarded in a local community not only for its grace in adorning a building but also for its timekeeping and sounding the hours.

A Typical Turret Clock Installation

To help those who may be new to turret clocks and to start introducing some necessary technical terms, let us take an imaginary visit to a turret clock in a church tower. Every tower is different, but this will serve to give a feeling of what is involved.

Entering by a low door at the bottom of the tower, we see in the cramped entrance, a gloomy stone spiral staircase winding its way upwards out of our sight. The steps are worn and uneven, narrow slit windows at every turn let in much-needed light, and it's rather cool and a bit dusty. An odd cobweb or two adds to the feeling that not many people pass this way.

The first door we meet opens into a room where the bell-ringers perform. Above us we can now just make out the muffled sound of the clock ticking, a steady deep clunk, rather like the sound of a very old grandfather clock, but deeper and slower. Swinging through a slot in the ceiling we can just see the bob at the end of the clock's pendulum. It is the size of a dinner plate, fairly thick, and held on to the pendulum rod by one of the biggest nuts we have ever seen.

Moving on up the spiral staircase from the ringing room we come to the clock room. The tick is now much louder and emanates from inside a large wooden clock case. Opening the case door we now see the clock itself, an iron frame filled with gear wheels; from the rear of the clock hangs the pendulum which we saw swinging in the room below. The clock mechanism is properly known as the 'movement'. More about how it works later, but what we can see of the movement seems to indicate that it is very old.

Right on the front of the movement is the setting dial so the hands can be set to time without having to see the outside dial, a bit unusual since on some dials the figures run backwards - and it only has one hand. A rod runs from the clock straight upwards to a set of gears on the ceiling above and from there another rod runs across the room to the back of the outside dial. A thin wire extends from the clock case to the ceiling, going right up to the belfry where it operates the bell hammer to strike the hours. Two steel ropes also come out of the clock case, pass upwards, over pulleys and then dive off into the dark corners of the clock room. Looking closer into these corners reveals that the lines have huge cylindrical weights hanging from them, each is about three feet tall, and a foot in diameter. These provide the driving power for the clock and for the striking as well. Below each weight is a hole in the floor, and it is down these holes that the weights descend— right down to the ground floor.

Looking up to where the rod reaches to behind the external dial, we see some gears, which drive the hour and minute hands. Small weights on the end of arms stick out at odd angles to counter-balance the weight of the hands outside. From this gearing on the wall a tube to the hour hand outside runs through a hole in the tower wall and inside it is a rod to drive the minute hand. In fact the hole is a small window, and the wall is very very thick; about four feet! A chink of sunlight from outside illuminates the back of the dial, it is green in colour, so we know that this dial is made from copper sheet.

Proceeding further up the staircase, we open another door and we are now in the belfry itself. Looking in we see the bells, dull green as seen in the sunlight streaming in through the louvres— the open slats which allow the sound to escape whilst keeping the rain out. Belfries can be very dangerous places, so we do not go inside, but just pause to look in. Suddenly a bell starts to sound, the clock is striking the hour. A few pigeons perched outside the tower are startled and take off, their wings making a frantic clapping noise. The note of the bell is very loud and deep, and since we are so close, it seems to be quite harsh. As the last stroke has sounded the bell goes on humming and humming, softer and softer until after a minute it has died away completely. Our visit is complete, we have discovered a turret clock.

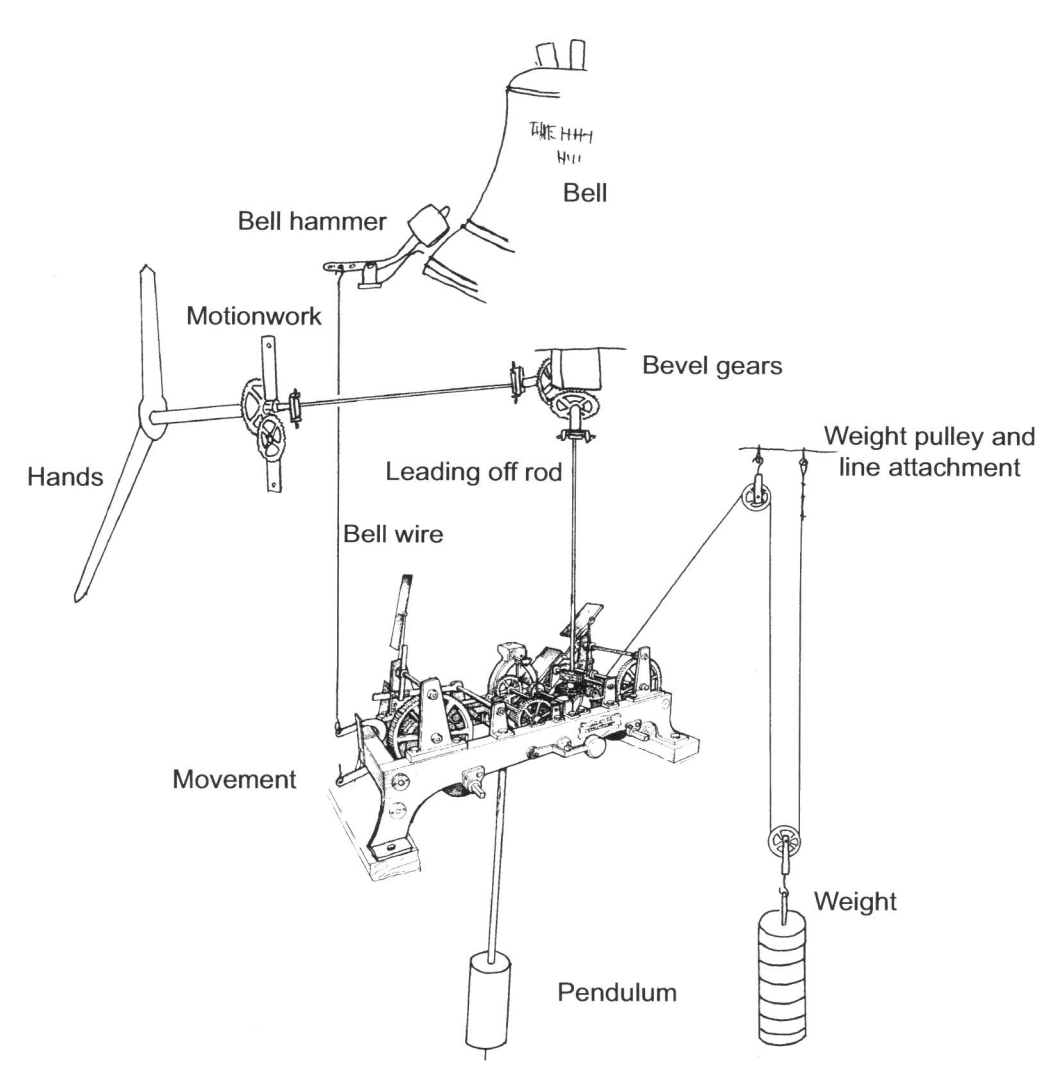

A turret clock installation

How a Turret Clock Works

A turret clock can have one, two, or three sets of gears called trains. The trains of gears are contained in a frame of iron. The first train is called the going train and this drives the hands to tell the time. The striking train operates the hour striking and the quarter train (sometimes called the chiming train) sounds the quarter hours. Each train is driven by a weight on the end of a steel line which is wound up round a wooden or metal barrel. On the barrel is a square on to which the winding handle fits. Since some clock weights can be more than half a ton, winding a turret clock can be very hard work.

Starting with the going train, the barrel has on it a large wheel called the great wheel, this drives a train of gears which could number two, three or four, depending on the design of the clock or how long it runs for. Each wheel is mounted on an arbor, the term for an axle; the pivots rotate in brass bushes and the small gears are known as pinions. In most going trains there is one wheel called the centre wheel which rotates once per hour. The last wheel in the going train, and the smallest, is called the escapement wheel or the escape wheel for short. This wheel rotates a lot faster than the others, usually it turns once in a minute. This is linked to the pendulum through the escapement, a device which allows one tooth of the wheel to escape for every swing of the pendulum. Without the escapement the trains of gears would run unchecked. So, as the pendulum beats time it controls the speed at which the escape wheel rotates, and hence through the train of gears with the appropriate numbers of teeth, it allows the centre wheel to turn once in an hour.

A pendulum swings with a regular number of beats per minute, the number depending only on the length of the pendulum. A pendulum about 39 inches long makes one swing in one second, but a pendulum about 14 feet long takes two seconds to make a single swing. In turret clocks most pendulums are somewhere between these two lengths. To reduce variations in timekeeping due to changes in length, caused by changes in temperature, some clocks have compensation pendulums. These are constructed using several different types of metal so that the pendulum remains the same length at different temperatures. Pendulums which have rods made of wood perform very well in different temperatures, but ones just of steel are not so good.

Let's take another look at the escapement since this important mechanism performs two tasks. Apart from releasing the escape wheel every swing of the pendulum and thus giving time to the clock, the escapement also gives the pendulum a little impulse every beat to keep it swinging. If it were not for this, the pendulum would not keep swinging and the clock would stop. The pallets are two little pads of steel which span the escape wheel and are connected to the pendulum by an arm called the crutch. The escape wheel pushes one pad until it escapes, the other pad then arrests the motion of an escape wheel tooth making the familiar 'tick'. Next the pendulum swings back, the second pallet releases a tooth and the first pallet again arrests the motion of the escape wheel making a 'tock' sound.

How does the clock drive the outside dials? Well, we have to return to the centre wheel which turns once per hour; it is this which drives the hands on the dials through a series of iron rods and bevel gears known as leading off work. Where the direction of the rod has to turn a corner, or where two or more dials are installed on a tower, bevel gears are used to change direction of motion. Each dial is driven by a leading-off rod which turns once per hour. Behind each dial is a cluster of gears known as the motion work, this takes the one turn per hour of the minute hand and drives the hour hand round once in twelve hours.

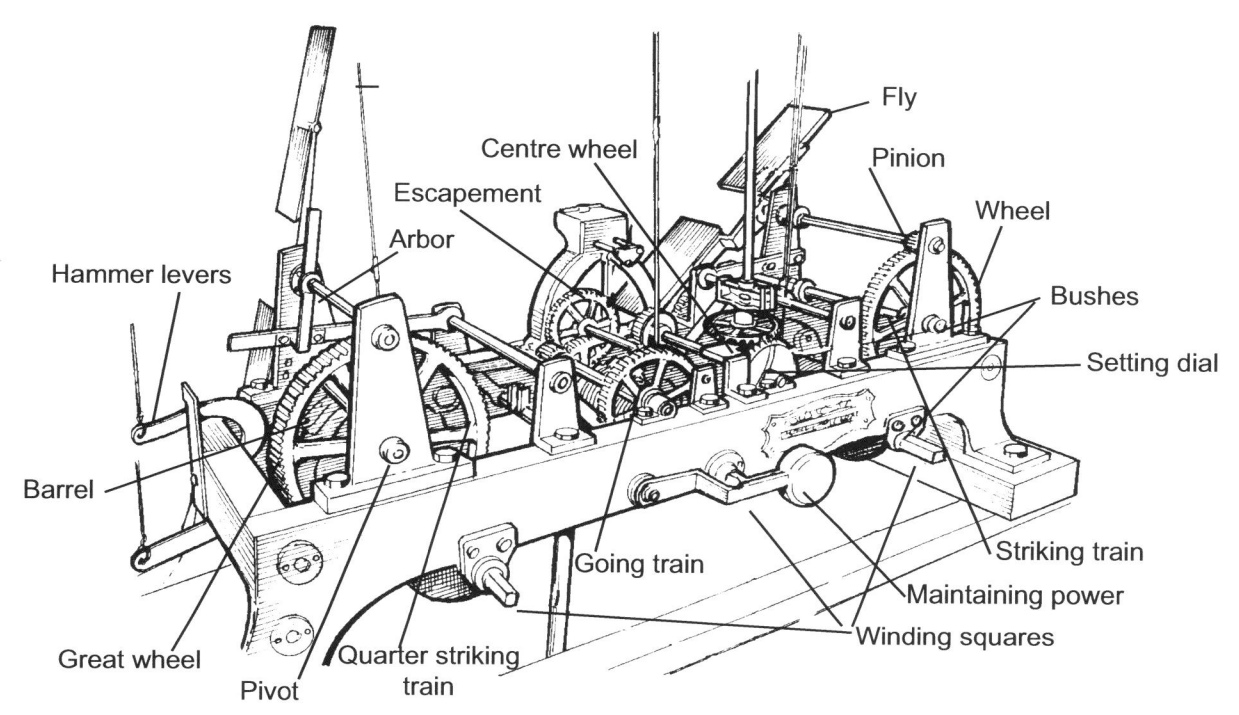

A three train turret clock movement circa 1890
(Artwork from the late David Nettell)

Most turret clocks strike the hour on a bell, it is the striking train which operates the bell hammer. A lever in the striking train is pulled down and released once for each stroke of the bell, this lever pulls a wire which runs to the belfry above the clock. Here it lifts a heavy hammer which then falls on the outside of the bell. A check spring keeps the hammer just off the bell so that once the hammer has struck, the bell can sound fully. If the bell is not directly above the clock, bell cranks are used to transfer the pull of the wire to the correct place. A few turret clocks have jacks who strike the hours, these are decorative figures whose arms are moved to sound the bells.

Both the going and striking trains are very similar. The striking train is also powered by a weight, but it is usually heavier than the one for the going train as it has to do more work. There is no escapement in the striking train, but a two-bladed fly revolves rapidly, its blades beating the air to control the speed of striking. In order to strike the correct number of blows one of two devices is used, a count-wheel or a rack. A count-wheel has notches at different intervals round its edge which are spaced so that the striking train will first run for one blow and stop. Then, when set off at the next hour, it will run for two blows and stop; and so on up to twelve o' clock. With rack striking, the rack, which looks like a section out of a gear wheel, is raised by one tooth every blow of the bell, until when it is fully raised, the striking stops. To control the correct number of blows the rack is allowed to drop the right amount by a specially-shaped cam called a snail.

Some clocks have a third weight and train of gears enabling the clock to sound every quarter of an hour; this is often called the chiming train, but a more precise name is the quarter striking train. As this has even more work to do, its driving weight is the largest of the three clock weights. Popular chimes are those called the Westminster quarters used in Big Ben or ting-tangs can be sounded on two bells. The quarter train is almost identical to a striking train; here the main difference is the number of bell hammers it operates.

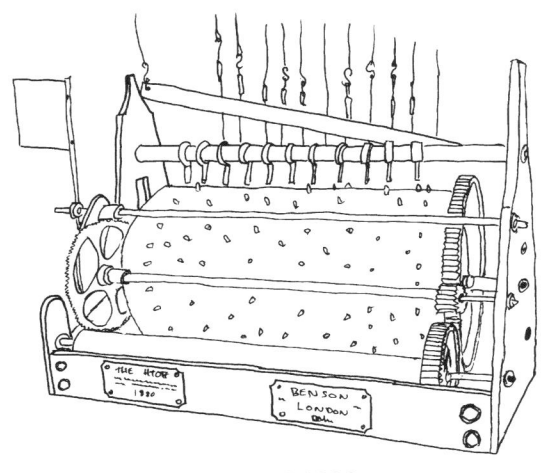

Tune barrel 1893

Another device sometimes connected to a turret clock was a tune barrel. 'Carillon' is a term often used to describe these devices, but strictly speaking a carillon is a set of 23 or more bells on which tunes can be played: so we will use the correct term of tune barrel. The tune barrel played tunes on the tower bells, hymn tunes were popular, as were national tunes and God Save the Queen— or King, as the case was at that time. Tune barrels are separate from the clock, look rather like a clock mechanism, but have a large drum with pins in which operate the bell hammers. The whole mechanism is rather like a huge musical box and is usually set off by the clock at certain times of the day. Sometimes the tunes change automatically, either for the different times of the day or for the different days of the week. In the 20th century carillons are sometimes found that are driven by compressed air.

Taking Care of a Turret Clock

Safety-- a Brief Introduction

Safety is an important issue today and rightly so. A clock tower can be quite a dangerous place to those unfamiliar with it and those responsible for the building must make sure that access to the clock is safe. Equally so, it falls to those who wind a clock to be resonsible for themselves and to highlight any safety issues that could affect them or others. As a guide, the following list shows common areas where safety can be compromised.

- Wooden ladders with worn / unsafe rungs
- Stone staircases with worn steps
- Vertical ladders not secured to wall and not enclosed with safety rings
- Rotten or wormed floors
- Poor lighting
- Old untested electrical installations
- Holes in floor (e.g. for weights to pass through)
- Platforms with no rails
- Clock weights and pendulums that people can walk under
- Unsecured trapdoors
- Pigeon droppings which can cause respiratory problems
- Danger from falling weight if a line broke
- Danger from falling pendulum if suspension spring broke

It is best not to work alone in a tower in case an accident happens or you get inadvertently locked in. If possible try to wind the clock at a time when there is someone around in the building maybe just after a service if it is in a church. Let someone know that you plan to be in the tower. When you have more to do than winding try to take someone with you. It is good safety practice and you may inspire another clock-winder too. A mobile phone is a useful aid.

Bells can be extremely dangerous when they are in the 'up' position; this is when the bell is supported mouth up. Just a small push and the bell comes off the balance and swings down crushing anything in its path. Those unfamiliar with bells should not enter a belfry when the bells are 'up', neither should any bell rope be touched. Bell ringers will normally leave a warning notice saying "WARNING! The bells are up". If you need access to a belfry discuss this with the tower captain or keeper.

Manual Winding

Wind the clock as required; this is likely to be daily, weekly, or sometimes two or three times a week, depending on the clock and how far the weights can fall. Most turret clocks have a winding handle which fits onto the winding square. Do make sure this is a good fit, because if it slips off injury could be caused to the person winding as well as damage to the clock.

Normally each train, going, striking and quarter striking if fitted, should be fully wound. It is best NOT to wind the quarter and hour striking trains when the clock is about to strike the hour or quarter. This is within the five minutes before quarter striking and ten minutes before the hour.

Wind until the weights are fully up; often a mark is painted on the line and used as an indicator; paint or white correction fluid is useful for this purpose and can be quickly repainted when it wears off. Always control the winding handle, allowing it to go backwards gently when winding is finished, thus lowering the click onto the ratchet to avoid any shocks and possible breakage. Do not begin winding too quickly, but start at a steady pace which can be maintained. It is vital that a weight is not wound too high. If it is then there is the danger of straining the line anchorage, forcing the line to come off a pulley, or at the worst, breaking the line and having the weight come crashing down. A weight of a quarter of a ton descending 30 feet will do considerable damage to anything in its way.

A maintaining power is a device which keeps the clock ticking whilst being wound, usually this is a lever which has to be pushed over to uncover the winding square. This type is known as bolt and shutter maintaining power. It is important to use it if fitted since it not only makes sure that the clock does not lose time during winding, but it also prevents damage to the teeth of the escape wheel.

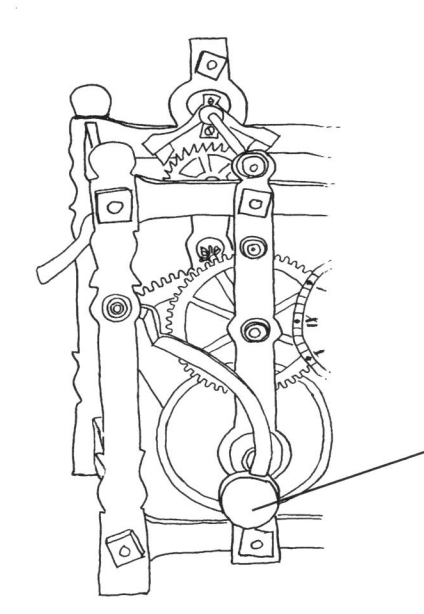

Bolt and shutter maintaining power circa 1780

There is a type of maintaining power, called Harrison's, which uses energy stored in a spring to keep the clock running. If you turn the winding handle backwards a little you can feel the spring tension up. Another type uses a system of epicyclic gears which are usually hidden inside the barrel; with these clocks the winding handle sometimes turns one way and the barrel turns in the opposite direction.

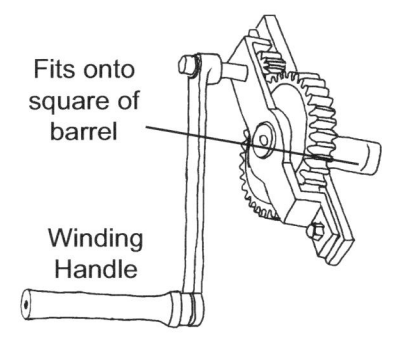

Large quarter or striking trains sometimes have a winding jack, this contains a set of reduction gears which make the clock easier to wind. Often the jack has to be put onto a winding square, and the winding handle then goes onto the jack. The frame of the winding jack butts against a stop, usually a wooden part of the supporting frame, to prevent it from turning. A variation of this is where the reduction gear is built into the clock; usually a pinion has to be engaged before winding and then disengaged after winding.

Winding jack late 19th century

WINDING GROUPS

The city of York has a winding club where a group of like-minded people wind the clocks. A charge is made for each clock but essentially the services are provided by volunteers. Money raised through winding fees is re-cycled to pay for maintenance, repairs and restorations. Since a group is involved a person only has a winding rota for say one week in a month or six weeks.

AUTOMATIC WINDERS

Some turret clocks are fitted with automatic winders which do away with the task of manual winding. They operate by an electric motor which winds up a small weight at regular intervals. In the event of a power cut, there is usually enough drop on the weight to keep the clock running for several hours. Some types use low voltage motors powered by a battery, these have a greater reserve and can wind the clock for several days without mains power.

Clocks with automatic winders still need regular care and attention. A visit, monthly at least, is necessary to check time keeping and set to time if necessary.

SETTING TO TIME

Most turret clocks have an internal setting dial which shows the time as indicated on the outside dials. They normally have just one hand to show the minutes, or sometimes a additional hand to show hours. Quite often the numerals on the setting dial run anti-clockwise.

There are several different systems for setting the hands; commonly used is a small key or spanner which fits onto a square on the setting dial, and when turned this moves the outside hands. Always use the spanner if there is one, because if you try to use the hand you are likely to bend or break it. A friction clutch allows the hands to turn, this is quite suitable for small dials, but where several dials, or large dials are used a different mechanism is employed.

A setting dial of around 1780. Use the setting spanner on the centre square to adjust the hands.

Those clocks which drive large dials usually employ a nut which has to be first unlocked to set the hands. Once this has been done, the drive from the clock is completely disconnected from the hands which can then be set easily to time. Once the dials indicate the correct time, the nut is of course locked up again. This system has the advantage that the drive is very positive and there can be no chance of the hands slipping.

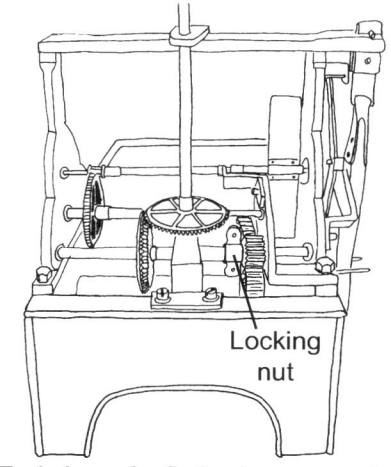

End view of a flatbed movement. 1880

An alternative to the nut is a dog-clutch where depressing a catch releases the hands to allow them to be set to time.

Press here to release hands

Dog clutch hand setting 1826

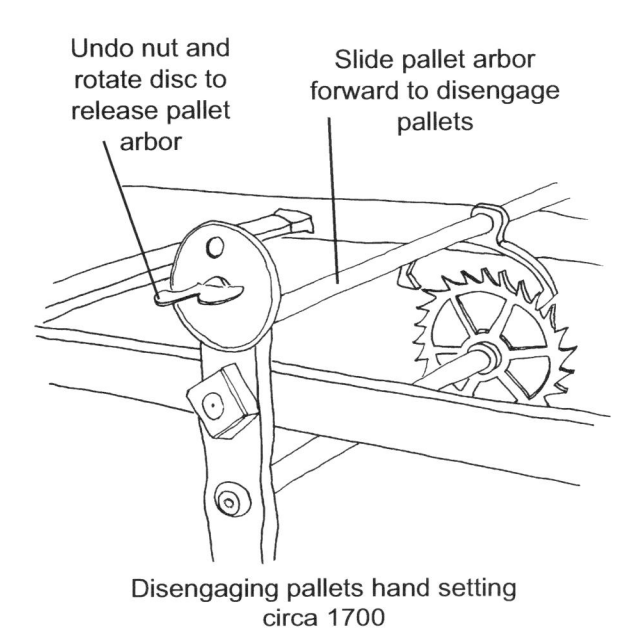

Undo nut and rotate disc to release pallet arbor

Slide pallet arbor forward to disengage pallets

Disengaging pallets hand setting circa 1700

Some 18th century clocks are set to time by sliding the pallets out of engagement with the escape wheel and letting the clock run forward. This must be done with great care since the escape wheel can easily be damaged. First stop the pendulum, but don't just make a grab at it as there is a lot of energy in the swinging bob; rather give it a number of small pushes to oppose its swing. Next push the catch which keeps the pallets in engagement to one side, hold the escape wheel arbor, and slide the pallets out of engagement. Allow the clock to run slowly forward by letting the escape wheel arbor run through your fingers. When you have reached the correct time (on no account let go, or let the wheel turn so fast you cannot control it), grip the arbor firmly to stop the wheel turning and slide the pallets back into engagement. Make sure the catch that retains the pallets is back into place. Finally, restart the pendulum by gently giving it a series of small pushes.

When setting a clock to time always turn the hands forwards and if you have to advance the hands past the hour let the clock strike fully. Should the clock have quarter striking, allow the chiming to finish after you set the hands past each quarter.

SETTING TO SUMMER TIME AND WINTER TIME

To set the clock to Summer Time advance the hands by one hour letting the clock strike at the hour and quarters.

To set the clock to Winter Time it is best to stop the clock for one hour by stopping the pendulum. Alternatively you can advance the clock by 11 hours letting the clock strike at every hour and quarter.

TO START THE CLOCK SHOULD IT HAVE STOPPED

Once the weights have been wound up, give the pendulum a small sideways push and keep pushing every swing until the clock starts to tick.

REGULATION

A well-maintained 18th century clock can still keep time to a minute or so a week, a Victorian clock with a pendulum compensated for temperature changes and gravity escapement may be within 5 seconds a week or better.

To get the clock to keep good time the pendulum may need to be adjusted. There is usually a large nut underneath the pendulum which can be screwed up or down to raise or lower the pendulum bob. Some clocks have a wing nut on top of the pendulum suspension bracket, which enables the suspension spring to be pulled up or down through a slot thus shortening or lengthening the pendulum.

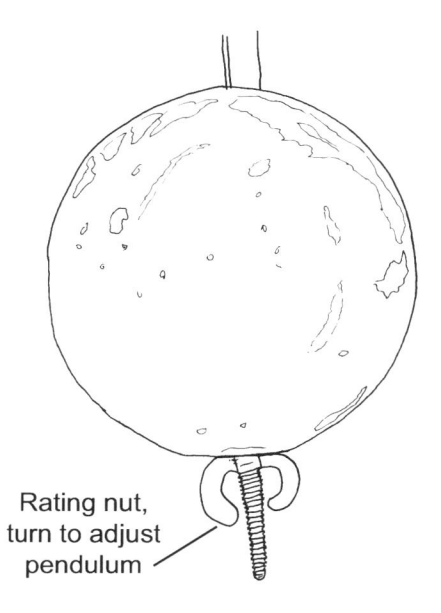

To make the clock gain, raise the pendulum bob.
    Turn the nut underneath the pendulum clockwise as viewed from underneath.

To make the clock lose, lower the pendulum bob.
    Turn the nut underneath the pendulum anti-clockwise as viewed from underneath.

Rating nut, turn to adjust pendulum

Bottom pendulum adjuster
circa 1700

Expect a change in time keeping of around half a minute a day to a few minutes for one turn of the regulating nut.

If the nut is underneath the pendulum first stop the pendulum. Do this carefully as some pendulums are very heavy (1 Cwt or more). Once the pendulum has stopped make the adjustment holding the bob so that you do not twist the whole pendulum and damage the suspension spring (the thin steel strip from which the pendulum hangs). On very heavy bobs it is worthwhile wedging a wooden block under the bob whilst making an adjustment; this stops the bob moving and saves your hand in the unlikely event of the suspension spring giving way. If the pendulum has not been adjusted for years the nut may have rusted and need releasing. A penetrating oil or dismantling fluid often helps to release seized up parts.

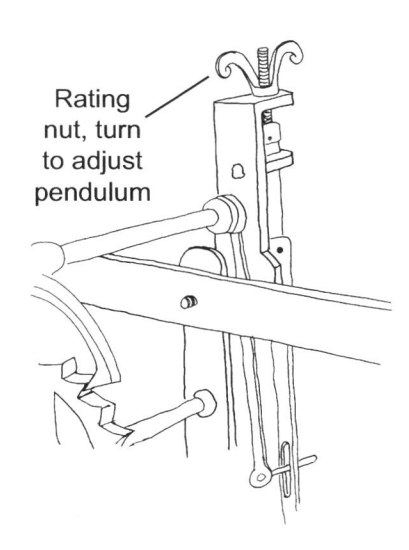

Rating nut, turn to adjust pendulum

Top pendulum adjuster
circa 1720

[23]

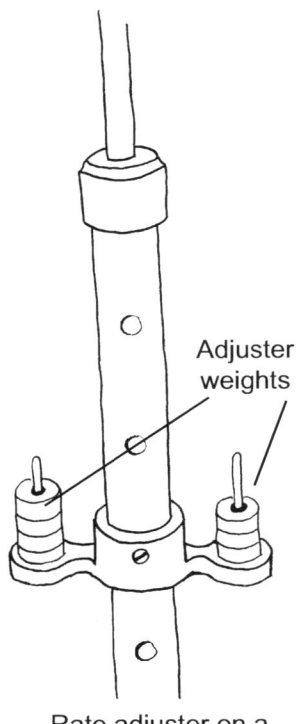

Some clocks, usually late 19th century clocks which have compensation pendulums, use small weights for fine regulation. These work by effectively raising the centre of gravity of the pendulum. Regulation weights are often in the form of large washers and slip on to one or two vertical rods close to the top of the pendulum. Sometimes people put a number of odd items on the top of a pendulum bob to help bring it to time.

To make the clock gain add regulation weights.

To make the clock lose remove regulation weights.

Expect a change in time keeping of a second or so a day for removing or adding one washer-type weight.

Rate adjuster on a compensation pendulum circa 1875

CORRECTING THE STRIKING OR QUARTER STRIKING

The striking may possibly get out of step with the time on the dial or the quarter striking may be out of sequence; this could be due to letting the clock run down and stop, inadvertently tripping the striking, or not allowing the clock to strike fully when advancing the hands.

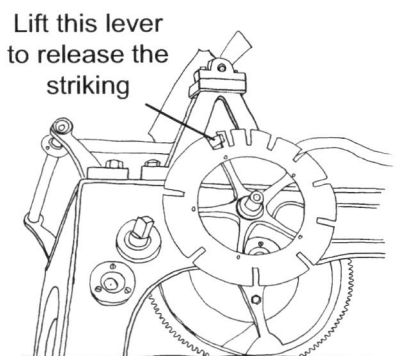

The clock may be corrected by setting off the striking or chiming. Most clocks have a count wheel to control the striking, this means the clock strikes 1, then 2, then 3 and so on. A count wheel has slots in its edge (or it may have pins that protrude), often they are marked 1, 2, 3 etc., and the spacing between the slots gets progressively longer. When striking has finished the correct number of blows a lever then drops into these slots which in turn stops the striking by locking the fly.

Striking train countwheel

Check the time on the outside dial, then lift the locking lever and let it drop. The clock will then strike. Repeat this process until the striking is back in step with the hands.

Note: The striking cannot be released if the clock has 'warned'. Warning is the clock's action just before it strikes. About ten minutes before the hour the going train partially releases the striking train, this is accompanied by a loud click. Exactly on the hour the striking train is released and the hour is struck. A quarter striking train warns about five minutes before each quarter.

Correcting quarter striking is much the same as correcting hour striking except that the locking plate normally only has four slots, one for each quarter. Sometimes the quarter locking plate will go round once every two, three or four hours, so it will have a multiple of four slots. For a chiming clock, correct the quarters first and then the hour striking since the quarters usually release the hour striking. Just to make things a little confusing, on both striking and quarter count wheels the first slot often runs into the second, so in these cases the striking countwheel only has 11 slots and the quarters 3 slots.

Note: Like the striking train, the quarters cannot be released if the clock has warned. In a quarter striking train, warning occurs about five minutes before each quarter.

Lift this lever to release the quarter striking

Quarter striking train countwheel

NIGHT SILENCING

Where the striking of hour and quarters through the night is considered antisocial, night silencing can be installed. Some old clocks in hospitals had this incorporated in their design. Today a modern night silencer can be added, this is usually an electric device which pulls the hammer clear of the bell so it will not sound; the times of the silent period are controlled by an electronic time switch.

BELL HAMMERS

Many turret clocks are in churches where there are rings of bells. Before the bells are rung, the clock hammers have to be 'pulled off'. A wire from the clock comes into the ringing chamber and this is pulled down and secured to a hook. The action is to pull the clock hammers well clear of the bells and their wheels, so that when the clock strikes the clock hammers will not hit and damage the swinging bells.

ELECTRICAL CLOCKS

From the early 1930s some dials were driven by synchronous electric motors. If there is a power failure then the clock will not tell the right time. Today automatic restart units are available which will keep the clock stopped for exactly 12 hours after the power failure, then they automatically restart the clock so it is back telling the right time. In another system, a power maintenance unit will provide mains voltage at the correct frequency from a battery-powered unit until the mains supply is restored.

EXPECTED TIMING PERFORMANCE

All clocks, both electronic and mechanical cannot keep 'perfect' time. They can in the main be expected to keep time within certain limits. The following figures give a sort of guide as to what to expect from a clock that is well maintained.

It is not uncommon to find a clock that will perform well for weeks or months and then its rate will change. There are two major factors that affect clocks; temperature and wind. Temperature changes the length of the pendulum rod, it gets longer as temperature increases. A clock with an iron pendulum rod that was keeping time in the summer at a temperature of say 25 °C will gain about 15 seconds a day in winter at a temperature of -5 °C.

Wood as a material for pendulum rods is less affected by temperature, for the temperature range suggested, the error is more like 5 seconds a day. However, wood will absorb moisture if it has not been well varnished and this will also cause an error. A compensation pendulum is made of tubes of iron and zinc and reduce temperature errors to near zero.

Wind has the effect or moving the hands, sometime adding to the driving force of the clock and sometimes reducing it. This varying force is transmitted to the escapement and this results in changes to timekeeping that are similar in magnitude to errors caused by temperature. The gravity escapement effectively eliminates the problems caused by varying forces due to wind.

A change in air pressure also causes a change in timekeeping, but this is a fraction of a second; quite small in comparison to other errors.

The following chart gives a sort of guide as to what performance a clock might give. It is assumed that the clock is in good condition and that weather conditions are steady with a constant temperature and no wind.

Clock	Escapement	Pendulum	Expected accuracy
17th century	Recoil	Iron rod	2 minutes a week
18th century	Deadbeat	Iron rod	1 minute a week
19th century	Deadbeat	Wood rod	30 seconds a week
19th century	Gravity	Compensation	5 seconds a week

Your Successor

Please try to cultivate a group of people who are able to look after your turret clock. In this manner the clock will be kept running despite one person being away, unwell or on holiday.

Turret Clock Terminology

This section is primarily intended as an aid to identifying the various parts of a turret clock not covered in the preceding text and to assist with filling in the Turret Clock Database Recording Form. It also gives a little history, particularly general dates as to when certain features on turret clocks were introduced. The dates are a guide only; anomalous styles do occur e.g. when a 19th century maker copies a 17th century clock.

Describing a turret clock

To describe a turret clock first detail the number of trains, then the frame type. followed by the escapement. The clock popularly called 'Big Ben' is thus a three train flat bed with gravity escapement.

Frames

Naming the frame and the escapement of a turret clock is a good way of classifying a movement. Commonly met frame types are detailed here, but other more unusual and less common types are encountered from time to time.

End to End Birdcage

The end to end birdcage frame is the earliest type. Here the trains are placed in line or end to end. Almost always the material is wrought iron, but occasionally wood is used. Its open frame gives rise to the term birdcage. Wedges or riveting hold the frame together; bars which carry the bearings are removable and held in by wedges. We know that clocks were in use in the 13th century and almost certainly this frame construction was used. It lasted up until the 1660s when the pendulum was introduced and the frame design changed putting the trains side by side. Most clocks of this type have been converted from foliot to pendulum.

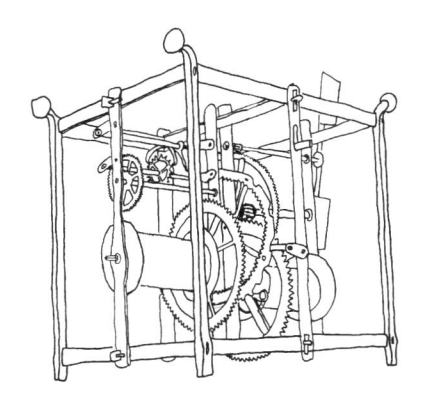

End-to-end birdcage movement probably 17th century

Side by Side Birdcage

Birdcage is the name given to the frame made of a cage of wrought-iron. Often the frame is held together by riveting or by screwed nuts. Individual bars that support the trains of gears can be removed and normally these are secured with nuts. The trains are placed side by side. This type came into use around 1670 and was used until cast iron superseded wrought iron at the end of the 18th century.

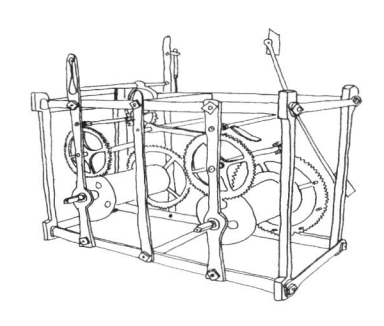

Birdcage movement circa 1700

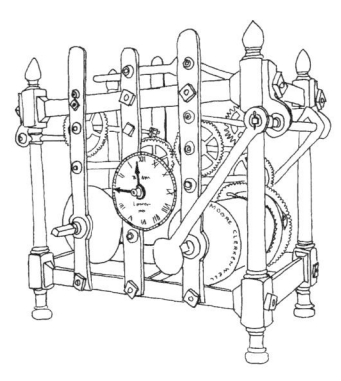

Posted frame circa 1830

Posted Frame

With the expanding availability of cast iron the posted frame became popular from around 1790; it lasted until the 1850s. Here all the frame and train bars were made of cast iron, usually the corner posts are either round or square in section. Generally, the parts bolt together, on smaller clocks the whole of the end frame is cast as one unit.

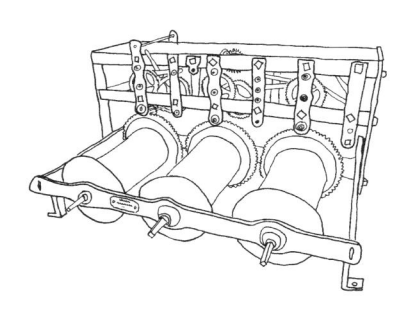

Double-framed movement of 1761

Double-Framed

Also known as extended barrel or sometimes colloquially called a chair frame or arm-chair, the double-framed construction comprises a short frame for the trains and long frame for barrels. In this way maximum strength is obtained whilst providing a long barrel which meant that many turns of line could be achieved giving a long going period. The period in which this frame was used is from 1730 to around 1860 and was popular with makers in Yorkshire, Derbyshire and Lancashire.

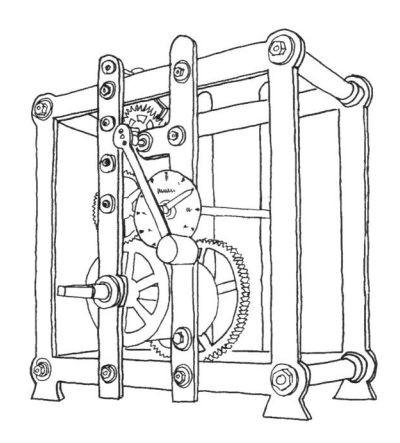

Plate and spacer movement of 1860

Plate and Spacer

Here was a variety which was easy to make. The plate and spacer frame comprised two cast-iron plates, one front, one back. These were held apart by four pillars. Train bars were removable in the normal way. Becoming popular around 1800, the design faded out after 1850, but continued to be used on small single-train clocks.

Flatbed

Becoming popular around 1850, the flatbed brought a major change to British turret clockmaking. A flat bed of cast iron was used as a base and wheel bearings and frames containing the wheels were then bolted onto this bed. Ideally it was possible to remove any wheel without disturbing another, but in reality this was seldom achieved. The Great Clock at the Palace of Westminster is an early flatbed movement.

Flatbed movement 1874

A Frame

Small timepieces of the 19th century often have a frame shaped like a letter 'A'; hence the term A frame. The picture of the clock with the Huygens automatic winderon page 35 has an A frame.

Wooden Frame

Wood was also employed for making frames, this tended to be used in a region covering East Anglia, Lincolnshire, Bedfordshire and Nottinghamshire and encompassed the last half the 17th century and first quarter of the 18th. These frames generally were of a vertical or 'doorframe' layout, but sometimes they mimicked the wooden birdcage construction. Just why wood was employed in these regions is not known, but was most probably a tradition.

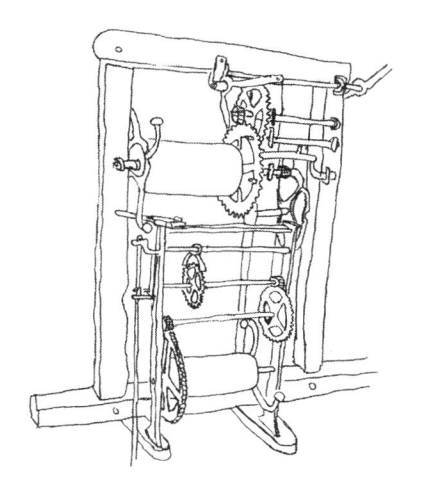

Woodframe clock with subsidiary iron frame for going train

Frame Materials

Wrought Iron was used in early clocks and can be identified by its uneven thickness, laminar structure and joints where another part has been fire welded on by the blacksmith. To make parts in cast iron first a wooden pattern is made, from this a mould is made in sand which is then filled with molten iron. Cast iron parts often have an intricate shape and sometimes a line can be seen where the sand mould was split. Some blacksmith work in wrought iron is so exact it is difficult to tell from cast iron.

Occasionally frames are made of brass, almost always on very small clocks.

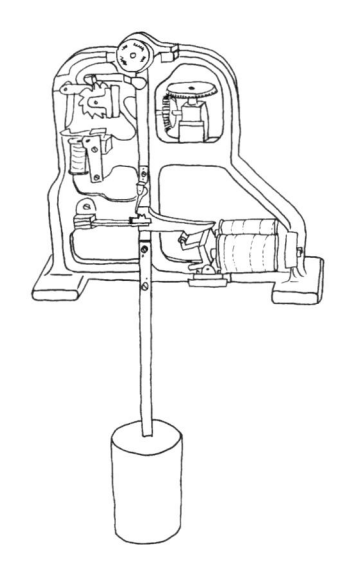

Electrical Turret Clocks

Waiting Train

This was really the first commercially viable electrical turret clock; it was patented in 1907. A heavy pendulum works as a motor and drives the dials advancing them by half a minute in about 25 seconds. The movement then stops advancing the hands and waits for a synchronising signal that is supplied every half minute from an electrical master clock. The signal releases the clock to go through another half minute cycle. The waiting train system is able to drive very large dials, some as large as 25 ft diameter

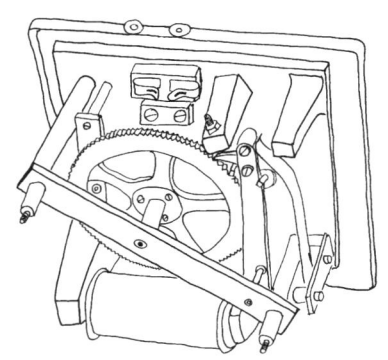

Waiting train movement circa 1930

Impulse Movement

Master clocks were introduced in around 1900; they produce an electrical pulse to drive slave dials every half minute. Impulse movements are used to drive small turret clock dials, the mechanism being situated behind the dial.

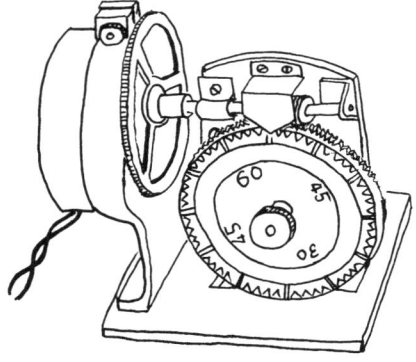

Impulse movement circa 1930
(Cover removed)

Synchronous Motor

Once the National Grid was established, voltage and frequency of the supply was standardised. A synchronous motor is driven by the 50Hz mains and its timekeeping is entirely set by the frequency of the supply which by law is set to close limits. The first synchronous motor driven turret clocks were installed in the early 1930s. Early synchronous clocks had to be started manually, they were not self-starting as later clocks were. Electronic backup systems are available to overcome power failure problems.

Synchronous movement circa 1930

Radio Controlled

Today many modern installations use electronic systems. Dials are driven by a motor controlled by very accurate time signals carried by radio transmissions from MSF Althorn. Changes between summer and winter time are automatic.

Escapements

The function of the escapement is to connect the pendulum to the clock; for every swing of the pendulum a tooth is released and the clock imparts a tiny impulse to keep the pendulum swinging. There are over 50 different types of turret clock escapement, but only four basic types are normally encountered.

Recoil

Introduced around 1670, the recoil escapement is commonly used on clocks of the 18th century. Use in the 19th century was usually confined to single train timepieces only. This escapement can be clearly identified by the escape wheel which, having been released, then moves backwards a little or 'recoils'. In this example the escape wheel turns anti-clockwise. The acting faces of the pallets are commonly curved. They are less likely to be damaged if the clock runs down and are very tolerant of wear, but reckoned by some to be poor timekeepers.

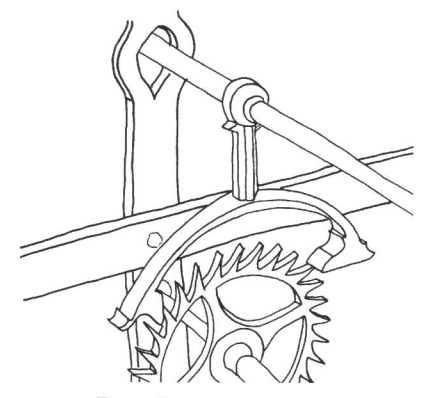

Recoil escapement circa 1680

Deadbeat

Invented in 1675, but not generally introduced until 1720, the dead beat escapement is used on high-quality 18th century movements. Its use in the 19th century was widespread. With the dead beat escapement the escape wheel advances, then stops 'dead', there is no recoil. In this example the escape wheel turns clockwise. If the clock weight runs down, there is a possibility that the teeth may be damaged when the sharp edges of the pallets butt onto the thin points of the escape wheel teeth.

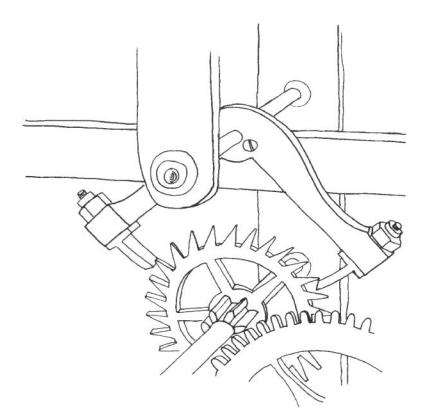

Deadbeat escapement circa 1740

Pinwheel

The pinwheel escapement is a variation of the deadbeat, pins on the escape wheel taking the place of teeth. Its use in English turret clocks starts in the late 18th century and was popular in the latter part of the the 19th century.

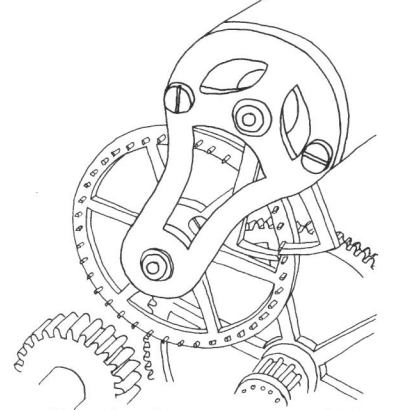

Pinwheel escapement 1918

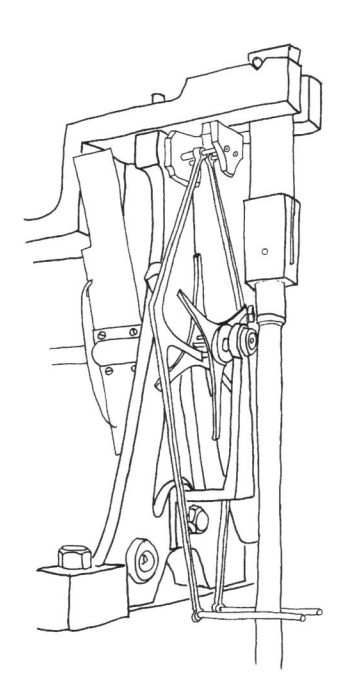

Double Three-legged Gravity

Invented by Edmubd Beckett Denison and employed in Big Ben in 1860, this escapement is used on high-quality clocks where accurate timekeeping is required. It is usually used in conjunction with a compensation pendulum. Here two arms are alternately lifted and released by the escapement. The escapement is very 'active', the escape wheel turning through one-sixth of a turn for every tick.

There are many variations of this escapement, but all have arms that impulse the pendulum.

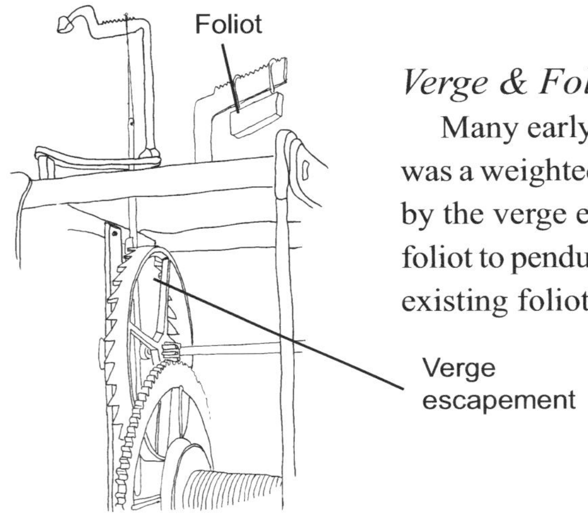

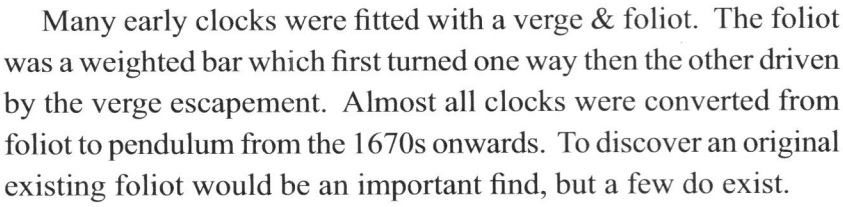

Gravity escapement 1878

Verge & Foliot

Many early clocks were fitted with a verge & foliot. The foliot was a weighted bar which first turned one way then the other driven by the verge escapement. Almost all clocks were converted from foliot to pendulum from the 1670s onwards. To discover an original existing foliot would be an important find, but a few do exist.

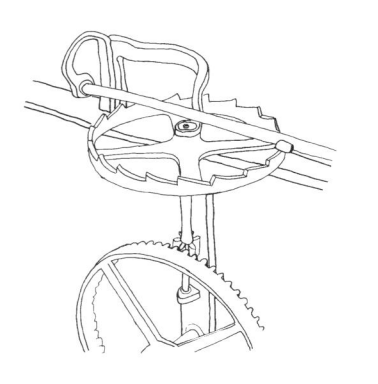

Verge escapement with foliot. Pre 1670

Verge & Short Pendulum

For a short period from around 1660 to 1690 some turret clocks were fitted with a short pendulum (about 2 ft long) and a verge escapement. These soon gave way to the long pendulum with a recoil escapement.

Verge & short pendulum circa 1690

Pendulums

The pendulum controls the timekeeping of the clock; it is the length that sets the time of each swing, not the weight. Generally the beat, the time taken to swing from one side to the other, is 1, 1¼, 1½ or 2 seconds. However some clocks have pendulums that have unusual beats. Common pendulum beats and lengths are listed below. The real length of a pendulum is slightly longer than the theoretical length.

Seconds per beat	Theoretical pendulum length	Beats per minute
1	39"	60
1¼	61"	48
1½	88"	40
2	156"	30

Early clocks had pendulums with iron rods. Wooden rods were used later to reduce the effect of temperature changes on timekeeping. In the 19th century compensation pendulums were used to near eliminate errors due to temperature variation. These pendulums employed two metals with different expansion rates and were usually constructed using concentric tubes. Often holes can be seen in the outside of the tube, the idea was to allow the air to access the compensation.

Weights, Lines & Pulleys

Turret clocks are driven by weights, though many have now been converted to automatic winding. Early clocks had weights made of stone and sometimes weights of lead can be found. Most commonly weights are made of cast iron. Before the 19th century these were cast as a single weight but by the mid 19th century a much more practical system had evolved. Here a central iron rod held small weights or 'cheeses' that could be slotted onto the rod where they fitted together. Cheeses were generally about 50lbs in weight so any weight could be easily made up.

Natural fibre rope was used for clock lines until around 1850 when steel patent line became available. This was invariably used on all clocks after this date and many older clocks that used rope had steel lines fitted as replacements.

Early pulleys for clocks with rope lines were made of wood with wrought iron bridles. Wood suffered from the attack of worm and today most clocks have cast iron pulleys.

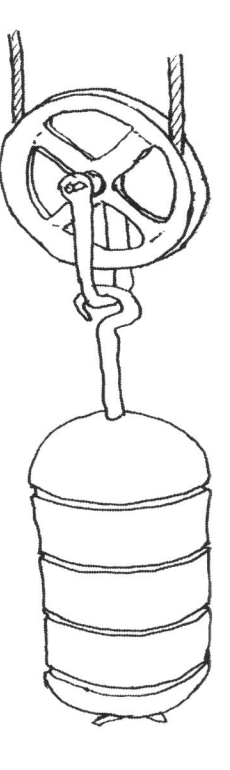

A going train weight. Each of the middle cheeses weigh 50 lbs

DIALS

Early clocks did not usually have dials; they only struck the hour on a bell. Dials when they did appear had only one hand, the hour hand. It was about 1700 when the minute hand appeared on turret clock dials. The driving force was probably the arrival of the recoil escapement with its improved accuracy plus society was becoming more sophisticated in its organisation.

Early one-handed dials were generally made of wood, were flat diamond-shaped and had a deep moulding round the edge. Lead flashing round the top prevented water from getting behind the dial. There were no minute marks but half hour or quarter hour makers were common. The hour hand usually extended just into the circle of chapters and had a decorative counterbalance. Often a sunburst or similar design was employed in the middle.

A lozenge shaped dial with single hand dated 1710

By the early 18th century copper sheet was readily available and the round convex dial became the norm for the next 150 years. Dials were invariably painted and the hands, minute marks and the Roman chapters done with gold leaf. A raised moulding round the edge gave strength in addition to the convexity of the dial. Hands invariable had a rib down them for strength.

Copper dial on a wooden tower. 1804. Note that IIII has been repainted as IV at some time.

By the mid 19th century cast iron dials became popular; these were skeletonised and often glazed with white opal glass and illuminated from inside by gas light. Sometimes a gas switch was driven by the clock to turn the gas on in the evening and off in the morning. Later electricity took over from gas.

Dials of stone, slate, lead or just painted onto a tower wall are also encountered. Sometimes the design of the hands can identify the clock maker from their distinctive style. It was not until the 20th century that 'modernistic' dials appear and all sorts were employed.

Late 19th century glazed skeleton dial set inside a stone moulding on a brick tower

In medieval times astronomical dials were provided in cathedrals and important churches. There are examples at Wells and Exeter. The latest of these astronomical dials was at Hampton Court Palace in the reign of Henry VIII.

Automatic Winders

Automatic winders are used to do away with the necessity of manual winding. In each type an electric motor re-winds a small weight at regular intervals. In the event of a power cut there is normally sufficient reserve to run the clock for several hours. Almost all systems employ a sprocket wheel connected to an arbor or barrel and roller chain to transmit power from the automatic winder to the clock. The weight used can be much less than the normal driving weight for the clock, but of course it has to be wound up more frequently. Early automatic winders were mains powered, but now some are battery powered, the battery being recharged from the mains. This method provides a reserve of several days whilst the mains-powered version, depending on its type and installation, may only provide a reserve of several hours. Battery-powered winders usually employ a small lead-acid battery that will need replacing after several years service.

The Church Buildings Council of the Church of England requires that automatic winders be connected to the great wheel or barrel arbor. This is a good practice. Where automatic winders are connected to second wheels then the second wheel is driving the barrel. Clock gearing is inefficient in this mode and severe wear can be caused in some circumstances.

All automatic winders should be fitted with a safety override switch. In the event of a fault where the winder fails to stop correctly, the override switch comes into action and turns the winder off completely to await maintenance. The override switch should not be reset until the cause of the fault has been identified and corrected.

The four basic types of automatic winder are:—

Huygens Endless Chain
A weight hangs on endless roller chain. One side of the chain provides driving power to the clock, the other is rewound by an electric motor when the weight has descended to a certain level. These were the first type used and the chain drive to the clock was connected to the second wheel arbor.

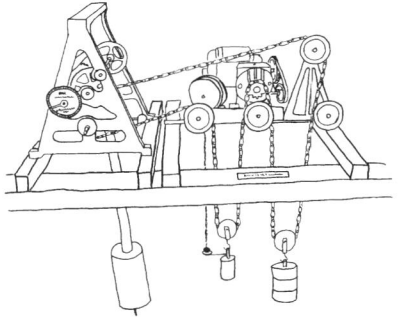

A Frame movement with Huygens auto winder

Monkey up the Rope
An endless loop of chain passes over a sprocket on one of the clock wheels. The motor hangs from one side of the chain and provides the going weight. The motor winds itself up the chain when it has descended to a certain level.

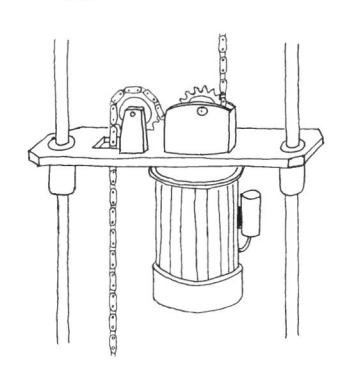

Monkey up the rope auto winder

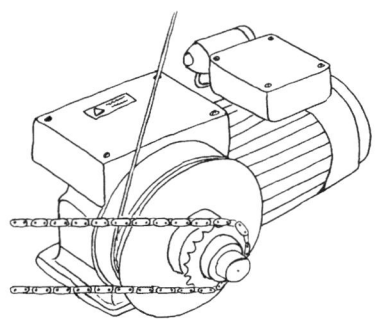

Differential (Epicyclic)

A differential gear has two inputs and one output. The output drives the clock, one input is a small weight on a line, the second input is from a motor. Periodically the motor rewinds the small weight after it has descended to a certain level. These are the most popular winders today they are a small size and can be positioned under, above or to the side of the movement. They can easily be connected to the barrel or great wheel.

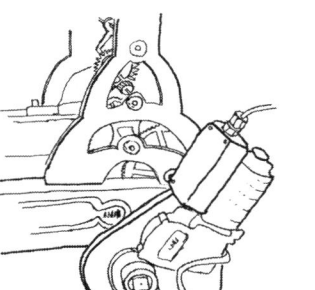

Epicyclic auto winder

Remontoire

The remontoire system has a weighted arm that is raised at regular intervals by an electric motor. As the clock ticks the weighted arm descends and a limit switch is actuated to turn the motor on and return the arm to its initial position. The system can bolt directly on to a winding arbor, but this could mean that the clock case would no longer close, or it would have to be modified to allow it to close.

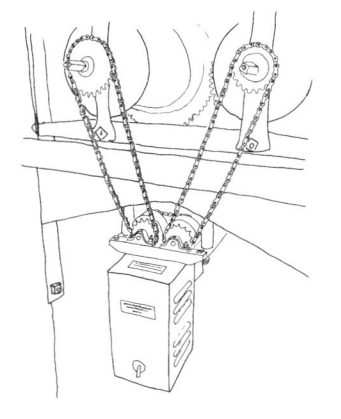

Remontoire automatic winder attached to a winding square

Power Assisted Winder

An electric motor winds up the original weights on the clock, this could be initiated automatically or under the control of an operator. Systems like this need to be very well designed so that undue strain and shock is not put on the clock. The advantage is that the clock retains the existing weights. However, problems with maintaining power and control means they are no longer used.

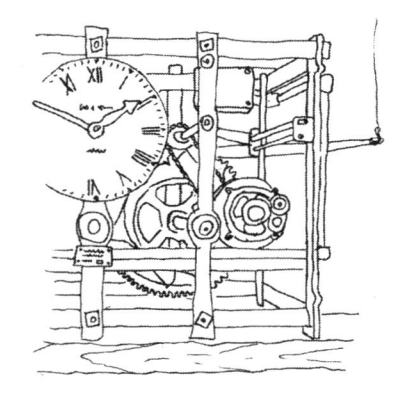

Power assisted winder

Direct Electric Drive

This system was once used for striking trains; it is not suitable for going trains. The fly was removed, an electric motor was connected to the fly arbor and the locking and release altered to incorporate switches. When the striking was initiated the motor ran and powered the train. The system is no longer used as the clock gearing was used in the opposite sense for what it was designed.

A direct electric drive where the whole train except the great wheel has been removed.

Night Silencing

In urban areas a clock striking through the night is unacceptable to some people. A night silencing unit can be installed to stop the bells ringing. This unit usually comprises an electrical linear actuator that is controlled by an electronic time switch. At a pre-set hour the actuator is turned on and this operates a wire that pulls the clock bell hammer clear of the bell. The clock carries on striking in the normal manner, but the bell is not sounded. In the morning the actuator is reversed and the clock bell hammer is lowered enabling striking to be resumed.

Clocks with heavy hammers have employed a similar system, but used a motor with gearbox reduction to obtain a similar result.

A useful solution is to arrange a device that holds up the striking release so that the striking train is left on the warning. The hold up is released 12 hours later and striking continues. A benefit of this system is reduced wear since the striking is only running for half the time. This application is best suited to clocks with countwheel striking.

Occasionally mechanical night-silencing can be found that was designed into the clock from the start. Such clocks were often adjacent to hospitals and date from the late 19th and early 20th centuries.

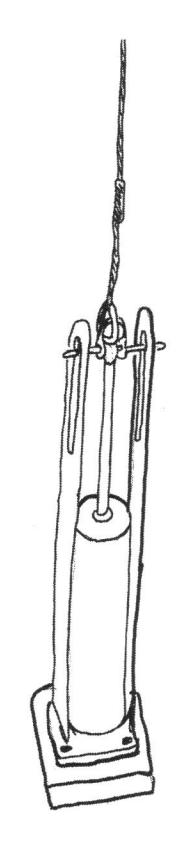

Night silencing linear actuator

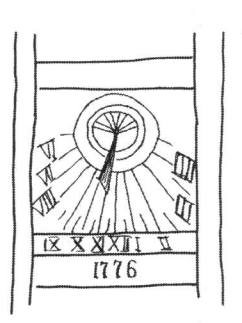

Automatic Correction

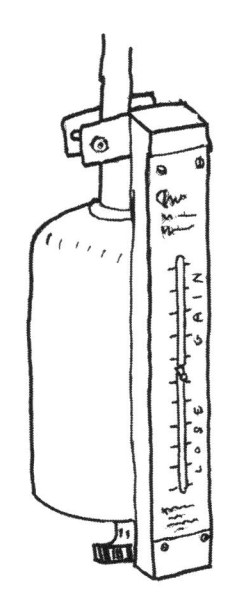

Sometimes it is very difficult to access a clock and having to crawl through roof spaces and climb vertical ladders is not uncommon. An automatic winder will keep a clock running, but the timekeeping of the clock will invariably drift leading eventually to an unacceptable error. Automatic correctors can ensure that a mechanical clock indicates the correct time. It is important to understand that correctors cannot ever remove the need for proper maintenance and care. Regular inspections of a clock are still required and might well reveal a problem; perhaps a leaking roof that would result in damage to the clock.

There are four systems in commercial use.

The first has a long box that is bolted onto the pendulum rod and connected to the electronics by a flying lead. Inside the box is a leadscrew driven by a motor and on the leadscrew is a weight. A microswitch on the clock is activated on the hour and the electronics assesses if the clock is within acceptable limits, fast or slow. If outside of limits, the weight is wound up or down to make an appropriate correction.

The second has a finger that from time to time touches the pendulum and thus assesses the rate of the clock. Corrections to speed up or slow down are made by the same finger retarding or or assisting the pendulum.

The third system employs an electromagnet below the pendulum that acts on a small magnet on the pendulum. By applying a current the pendulum can be made to gain, the electromagnet field assisting the force of gravity. By reversing the current the pendulum can be made to lose the magnetic field reducing the effect of gravity. A switch on the clock signals the hour and the electronics makes the appropriate corrections.

The last system is a pendulum catcher that is an electro-mechanical device that arrests the pendulum at the extreme of its swing and holds it there. The catcher can be used to correct a clock or used to stop a clock for 1 or 11 hours in order to set the clock backwards or forwards for winter and summer time. The catcher works in conjunction with control electronics that have a time reference from radio transmissions.

Pendulum regulator leadscrew and weight

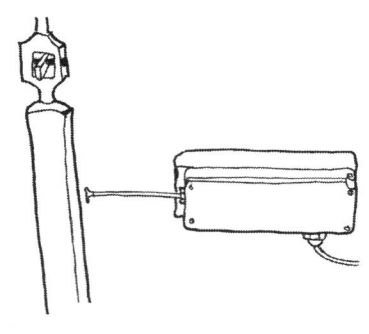

Pendulum regulator, pusher type

Pendulum catcher showing the pendulum arrested. The horizontal catcher arm is normally in a vertical position.

Electro Hammers

Traditionally a bell is struck by the clock operating a hammer on the outside of the bell. A wire goes from the clock striking train to a hammer fixed close to the bell. In operation the clock raises the hammer and then releases it allowing the hammer to fall on the bell's soundbow thus sounding the bell. New installations of clocks, Angelus striking, tolling for services, tolling for funerals, and carillons invariably employ electro hammers.

An electro hammer comprises a pivoted hammer and an operating electro-magnet. A short pulse of power (usually mains voltage) to the unit causes the hammer to turn and strike the bell. A counterbalance inside the electro hammer returns the hammer to the neutral position.

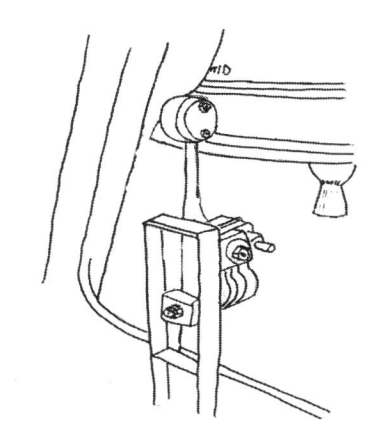

An electro hammer installed on a bell

Electro hammers have the advantage of being fairly small and compact compared with conventional hammers. These hammers can be easier to install; since they only require an electrical wire to be run to each hammer, there is no need for steel wires and bell cranks.

Occasionally, electro hammers have a use in traditional installations. One example is when a ring of bells has been augmented say from 8 bells to 10 bells and the new frame does not allow sufficient room to re-use the old clock hammers. In such a case, fitting electro hammers might be a solution to be considered. Switches may be added to the clock and these would be operated by the mechanical hour striking or quarter striking cams. The switches would then activate the electro hammers. However, electro hammers should only be considered when the possibility of using mechanical hammers has been properly investigated.

Whilst a heavy clock hammer will bring out the full range of notes of a bell, electro hammers are thought to be less capable of producing a good note.

Turret Clock Maintenance

Turret clocks have to perform in a hostile environment as often towers are cold, damp, dusty and windy. Basic maintenance is essential to keep the clock in good condition and performing well.

Basics

The purpose of this section is to enable those responsible for the care of a turret clock, to plan the maintenance of that clock. It is not intended as a do-it-yourself guide since many of the operations need to be done by a professional person experienced in turret clock work. Errors in maintenance could lead to damage to the clock, bells, bell wheels, the building structure, injury to the person winding the clock or to persons in the vicinity. The points presented here are to make the turret clock keeper aware of the aspects involved. As each turret clock installation is different, turret clock keepers are strongly advised to take professional advice concerning the maintenance of their clock.

An eight day quarter striking turret clock with 4 dials needs lubrication in over 100 different places. Clocks have been damaged by people who have oiled or greased wheel teeth; dust and grit sticks to the oil to make an efficient grinding paste which rapidly wears pinions.

Protection is better than a cure, so a good wooden case (which can be locked) round the clock will protect it from dirt. Likewise, it is a great advantage to have a protective box over the motion work behind each dial and another around the bevel gears in the leading off work.

The best scheme is that a turret clock should have an annual service from an experienced professional who would perform the following tasks:—

Safety Checks

Make a safety check on…
- Weight lines
- Weight line attachments
- Pulleys
- Flys
- Striking and chiming fly clicks
- All barrel clicks
- Suspension spring
- Bell hammer adjustments
- Bell hammer pull offs
- Dial fixing

Wipe off excess oil and dirt from...
- Clock movement
- Leading-off work
- Motion work
- Bell hammers and cranks

Lubricate the...
  Clock movement
  Leading-off work
  Motion work
  Bell hammers and cranks
  Wire lines

CLEANING

During a maintenance visit cleaning will involve removal of any excess oil, grease and dirt. It would not cover major work requiring the dismantling of the clock or other parts which would be required in a full overhaul or restoration. Cleaning is done with rags and dirt in wheel teeth and pinion leaves is brushed out with a stiff paintbrush.

It is recommended that a turret clock be stripped down and cleaned every 10 years.

LUBRICATION

Where oil is needed turret clock oil is used. Engine oils are unsuitable as they are designed for operation at high temperature and pressure and they have many special additives and detergents. Cycle oil and sewing machine oil are too light. Grease is used where sliding contact occurs.

Clock movement

Every rotating pivot is oiled, also pivots on levers. The escape wheel is the only wheel where the teeth are oiled in a turret clock as there is a sliding action between the wheel teeth and the pallets. There are parts on the clock which need lubricating, but are not as obvious as the pivots on the front of the clock. There are of course all the pivots on the back of the clock as well as places which are hidden from view like the barrel clicks, centres of the great wheels, clicks on the flys, and the flys. A professional will be aware of where and where not to apply lubrication and how much to apply. The enthusiast is likely to put oil in the wrong place and use too much leading to sticky patches that attract dust and dirt.

Leading-off work and motion work

Rotating parts on the motion work and bevel gears all need oiling. Since these parts are usually much more exposed to the weather they need greater care to ensure the clock works properly. Sometimes long leading-off rods are supported by rollers or hangers; these too will need lubrication.

Bell hammers and cranks

All bell cranks and hammers pivots need oiling. The hammer check spring should be greased where it supports the bell hammer. Towers that have bells for ringing usually have a tower keeper who looks after the maintenance of the bells. They might maintain the clock bell hammers as well. It is worth checking to clarify who is responsible for the clock hammers.

Wire lines

The life of wire lines can be extended by lubrication. Special wire rope lubricants are available which are between an oil and a grease, they not only lubricate, but also repel moisture. Make sure the whole length of the line is lubricated including the standing end and that out of sight inside weight chutes.

Record Sheet
It would be useful if a log sheet or note book were kept with the clock in its case. This could be used to record the winder's name, address and phone number, any maintenance performed and problems encountered. Another function would be to record the clock's rate and what adjustment was made to the pendulum. In this way the keeper would soon get to know exactly what effect on the timekeeping one turn on the rating nut would have.

Basic preventative measures
First a good clean up is the order of the day. To keep birds out netting can be applied on the inside of the louvres. Beware that pigeons are sometimes called the 'rats of the air' and carry many diseases. It's best to get a professional firm to clear an infestation, but even if you decide to clean away a few old nests first find out about the health hazards and if you go ahead, wear full protective clothing and face masks.

Sets of bevel gears and motion work should be protected from dirt by wooden boxes, if none exist then have some made, it is an excellent low-cost method helping to keep the clock running. Plywood is more than adequate and the boxes are easy to make.

Likewise a case round the clock will greatly reduce dirt and dust. Bare stone and brick walls shed grit that is very damaging to a clock mechanism. Application of a stabilising solution may help reduce the dust problem. If you make a new case make sure that all the sides can be removed to give easy access to the clock for servicing.

What to do if the Clock has Stopped
A clock may stop for a variety of reasons; the common causes are: the weights have run down, there is a problem with the leading off work, motionworks or hands, or possibly the striking may have jammed.

First make sure that all the clock weights have been wound. If you can see a weight has reached the ground then that may be the problem. If the weights are out of sight just a wind few turns on each train to check what is going on. Start the pendulum by giving it a series of gentle pushes until the clock starts to tick. If the tick is firm and strong then the clock is running, if it is weak and hesitant then something is wrong and further investigation is needed.

Try advancing the hands, if trying to move them gives more resistance than normal then it indicates some problem with the dials and hands, leading off work or motion work. Suspect something like bird nesting material in the motion work. If it is impossible to move the hands forwards, try moving them backwards by 5 minutes or so and see what happens then. Do not force them if resistance is felt. Some clocks will jam up if the striking or chiming weights have run down, but the going train is still running. If the striking starts then this might clear the problem.

Basic Diagnostics

If a clock has stopped there are some basic diagnostics that can be performed that might help locate the source of the problem. Where a clock has automatic winders note the position of the going train winder weight. If this is fully down, then there is likely to be a problem with the automatic winder. If fully up suspect a long power cut causing the clock to stop. Battery-powered winders do not suffer from this problem.

If the clock will not tick then take hold of the pallet arbor and try to slide it back and forward. There should be at least 1mm endshake and some slight resistance felt if there is power on the train. Next do the same with the escape wheel. If easy to move then this is indication that power is not reaching this wheel. Continue down the train of gears to try to locate where the power is being lost. Unfortunately these tests take an element of skill in knowing what resistance to feel for. For a barrel it is usually impossible to do this test.

If these basic checks fail, or if the clock is in the habit of often giving problems then it is time to call in an expert to help you. To help them keep a record of when the clock stopped giving dates and times. Leave the clock in its stopped state so the clockmaker can examine the installation when they call.

Dials and motionworks

Motionworks are situated behind the dial and provide the 12:1 reduction needed to drive the hour hand. This needs as much care as the clock does since it is in a very exposed situation and prone to corrosion and dirt. When a turret clock stops, about 50% of the time the problems are with the leading off work and motionworks.

Unfortunately if motionwork needs to be dismantled for a complete overhaul the hands need to be removed. This requires approaching the dial by rope access, by scaffolding or by a hydraulic platform. If ever any building work is taking place that employs scaffolding or platforms, then get a clockmaker to remove and overhaul the motionworks at tghe same time.

Restoration and Conservation

Conservation is a discipline that has been used in the museum world for a long time. Only recently clock restorations are being carried out with conservation in mind. Conservation has more than enough special jargon of its own. However, it is worth getting to grips with the key terminology since grant-awarding bodies are likely to favour a conservation-minded approach to planned work.

Terminology

Cultural-heritage is a term met at every turn in the Conservation world; a definition is… Cultural heritage, national heritage or just 'heritage' is the legacy of physical artefacts (cultural property) and intangible attributes of a group or society that are inherited from past generations, maintained in the present and bestowed for the benefit of future generations. Cultural heritage includes tangible culture such as buildings, monuments, landscapes, books, works of art, and artefacts, intangible culture such as folklore, traditions, language, and knowledge, and natural heritage including culturally-significant landscapes, and biodiversity.

Conservation is the deliberate act of keeping cultural heritage from the present for the future. The activity of Conservation can be further elaborated to be any methods that prove effective in keeping that property in as close to its original condition as possible for as long as possible.

Intervention means doing something to the object. An intervention could range from a non-invasive activity, like introducing environmental control round the object to a full cleaning and execution of actions to stabilise, strengthen and prevent deterioration.

Preventive Conservation is an activity to minimise decay, deterioration or loss. Examples are typically security, environmental control, storage, handling, packing and transportation. To this can be added, education. There a great benefit to educate the winder of a turret clock on its history and correct management as well as educating the carers and owners.

Remedial Conservation is a measure aimed at arresting current damaging processes or reinforcing the structure of an object. For a turret clock this might involve painting bare metal or replacing dial fixings. As such these operations alter the current state of the clock.

Restoration is a word loosely used in horology where it is generally applied to any repair, replacement or cleaning operation. The European Confederation of Conservator-Restorers' Organisations (ECCO) has a precise definition: Restoration consists of direct action carried out on damaged or deteriorated cultural heritage with the aim of facilitating its perception, appreciation and understanding, while respecting as far as possible its aesthetic, historic and physical properties.

Since Conservation so often goes hand in hand with Restoration, the general term *Conservation-Restoration* encompasses these two sometimes opposing philosophies, that may be broadly stated as keeping the clock in working order with minimum loss of original material. Turret clocks are expected to work 365 days a year, tell the time with reasonable accuracy, strike on a bell or bells and show the time on a dial that is clearly legible. Balancing restoration and conservation demands a professional approach. On one hand there is preservation, on the other the need to have a working clock. Decisions on what to do need to be backed with reasons.

STATEMENTS OF SIGNIFICANCE AND NEED

So, anything from the past is cultural heritage, but how old, or important, should something be before it is regarded as deserving of being preserved for the future? And, what should be done to achieve the preservation? The answer lies in a Statement of Significance and a Statement of Needs.

STATEMENT OF SIGNIFICANCE

The *Statement of Significance* summarises a cultural-heritage item to combine technical details with social history to give a pithy description thus turning an isolated artefact into an object that people can relate to. The Statement also gives an indication of the rarity, importance or uniqueness of the object. These statements are very useful when applying for grant aid from heritage bodies. The Statement of Significance originated in Australia and is now a commonplace requirement in Heritage projects. A search on the internet will reveal advice on preparing a Statement.

As far as a turret clock goes it is the technical details of the movement, plus the dial, the building it is in, the clock case, weights, pulleys and weight shafts. Add to this history about the maker, donors, repairs and how the clock fits into the local culture and you start to see that a turret clock is much more than a movement.

STATEMENT OF NEEDS

The *Statement of Needs* is all of Rudyard Kipling's Six Honest Friends; how, what, why, where, when and who. Add to these Ebenezer Scrooge's management team of budget, cost, payment, timescales and warranty and we have a sufficient starting point to define what is desired for a turret clock.

A statement of need is a document that evolves as more information becomes available. In its final state the statement should give information on possible courses of action that have been considered and an explanation as to why the preferred option was chosen. In this manner the need can be clearly identified and understood.

A good statement is particularly important when applying for a church faculty or applying for grant aid and a short well-presented document is better than a long one that contains unnecessary detail.

RESTORATION AND CONSERVATION POLICY

Any person who undertakes work on a turret clock should subscribe to the spirit of the following policy in order to preserve the clock for future generations.

No parts should be removed from the clock.

The clock should be preserved in its historic form as much as possible. This includes past alterations such as conversion from foliot to anchor and old paint coverings.

Repairs should be sympathetic and fit in with the character of the clock.

Additions, such as automatic winders, must always be effected without removing any of the original parts of the clock and so they can be removed without trace. No parts should be cut or drilled: attachments should only be made by clamping to the framework.

Repairs and restorations are always a compromise with conservation and it can be difficult to decide exactly what to do. To replace a badly damaged escape wheel on a 17th century clock may be justifiably necessary to keep the clock running. However, to conserve the original wheel, an expert can replace a damaged tooth or fit a brass band round the wheel into which the new teeth are cut. To replace every iron wheel in a 15th century clock, if they were badly worn, would be unwise as so much ancient history would be lost.

BEYOND ECONOMIC REPAIR

Sometimes a clock is said to be "beyond economic repair". In the main such a statement has to be carefully questioned. Facts should be given as to what the problems are and what is to be the likely cost of repairing the clock. Any clock can be repaired given sufficient funds, but of course that might transform an old clock into a modern artefact.

Sadly such statements can be used when the clock creates an embarrassment, say where bells are re-hung and no consideration was given to the clock. Supplying a new electronic clock might be an easy solution for a non horological person. A clockmaker or company that has limited facilities or relevant skills might be tempted to use the "beyond economic repair" ticket. They too might find supplying an electronic clock the easiest solution.

If a non-specialist has said the clock is "beyond economic repair" then the opinion of a professional turret clock restorer MUST be sought. If a turret clock company thinks a clock is "beyond economic repair" it would be most wise to seek the opinion of another turret clock restorer.

Sometimes the "beyond economic repair" ploy is used to justify something modern that can be "fitted and forgotten". Doing a 'lifetime cost of ownership' estimate is a very useful exercise. This compares the overall cost of different options over the lifetime of the equipment and considers initial cost, warranties, running cost and maintenance.

In the case of Church of England churches or a heritage organization, the retirement of a mechanical turret clock is seldom sanctioned. If sanctioned, the clock movement must be retained in the building.

DIALS

Dials are ephemeral. Painting and gilding could last from 20 years to 50 years or more depending on how the work was done, materials used, which way the dial faces and weather conditions. Each time a dial is repainted it can lose some of the accuracy of its original layout. Often the old chapters and minute marks are scratched around onto the copper dial, but the restorer then finds that other clockmakers have done the same leaving a mass of conflicting information. When a dial layout looks clumsy it is probably best to start afresh and to do a new layout in an appropriate classical style.

Colours used in painting clock dials are usually black or blue; traces of earlier paints can be found to identify previous colours. The chapters and hands are then gilded with gold leaf; 23½ carat or 24 carat being the best. On no account try to substitute gold paint for gold leaf; this turns brown after a few years and is a false economy. Occasionally dials are encountered that are not gilt. Black chapters on a white dial, or white chapters on a black dial were used, probably for economy.

When dials are repainted it is a good practice to record what layers of colours, finishes and layout marks were encountered.

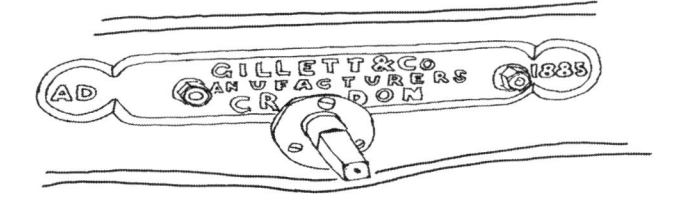

Commissioning Turret Clock Work

Major work on turret clocks is only needed on an occasional basis, so those commissioning such work may well be unfamiliar with the various issues. The objective in this section is to highlight topics that are important so that both the owner and the restorer understand exactly what is expected.

When a turret clock needs attention it may be as a result of different situations. Commonly encountered are…
> The clock is in poor condition, it may not run or has several faults.
> The clock has a specific fault or is unreliable.
> Getting someone to wind the clock is a problem, an automatic winder is required.
> The clock needs to be moved as part of a tower reorganisation / re-hanging of the bells.
> The dials are in poor condition and need painting and gilding.

Deciding what is needed

An ideal starting point would be a Statement of Significance and a Statement of Needs. In reality such statements evolve as a result of suggestions provided in quotations from clockmakers in addition to the obvious requirement. At the very least a list of needs should be provided; this can be broken down as in this example below. In this way a structured and itemised quotation can be produced. Churches would find it useful to involve their diocesan clocks adviser at an early stage to avoid pursuing a course of action that cannot be supported at a later stage.

Essential
    Clock repaired and overhauled
    Striking working

Desirable
    Automatic winders
    Night silencer

Will need doing at some time when funds allow
    Paint and gild dials

Requesting a Quotation

You will need to meet the clockmaker on site to explain what you think you need. A qualified professional will be aware of issues that you might not have considered. Access will be needed to the clock, weights, bell hammers and gearing behind the dial. Make sure that any bells are safely in the 'down' position. It is useful to involve the clock winder or carer and tower keeper or ringing captain when bells are involved.

Some restorers might ask for a fee for preparing a report. This is not unreasonable since it might involve them in a day's work plus travelling expenses. Some restorers will give a free report. Make sure you know if a charge is payable before requesting a site visit.

Ensure you agree a suitable validity for the quotation, this would probably be based on a typical timescale for committees to meet, consider proposals and in the case of churches, apply for a faculty. and perhaps raise funds.

It is wise to seek several quotations where the work involved may be more than a small repair.

If the building involved is a secure location, like a prison, or the maintenance is through a third party, then the clockmaker must be made aware of the access issues since this will add a cost to the quotation.

WHAT A QUOTATION SHOULD CONTAIN

A well-prepared quotation should contain the following information: -

A description of the clock covering historical and technical information.
An indication as to the clock's historical importance.
An assessment of the current condition of the clock.
A detailed proposal of the work that should be carried out.
Clear pricing showing different options if necessary
Clear statement about any exclusions.
Estimate of work that might need doing but cannot be properly assessed.
Statement of quotation validity.
Warranty information.
Information on what sort of report would be provided on the work carried out.
A statement about public liability and insurance on goods out of the building.

REASONABLE EXCLUSIONS

The clockmaker is likely to put exclusions in a quotation and in the main they should be reasonable. They can be used to highlight areas where it is not possible to anticipate exactly what is needed, or work outside of the clockmaker's control.

Examples are:
Supply of electricity for an automatic winder.
Building work needed on masonry or stonework.
Carpentry work, say on beams discovered to have woodworm.
Provision of scaffolding or hire of cherry picker to access dial.

For items specifically relating to the clock there are some areas that cannot be inspected accurately.

Dials, dial fixings and hands (unless accessed via scaffolding or rope)
The minute hand arbor and the hour tube cannot be inspected until the hands have been removed. Sometimes these will need work doing on them.

However, estimates can be given that cover the likely cost of work involved in the event of such problems being found.

Very occasionally after cleaning other faults show up, e.g, a crack in cast iron wheel that was once covered with grease and grime. Deeply scored pivots are another possibility. Such cases are unusual but even the experienced turret clock restorer can miss items like these. In such cases during work in progress the clockmaker should raise the issue with the customer for sensible discussion.

UNREASONABLE EXCLUSIONS

Some exclusions listed in a quotation may be unreasonable. A restorer may put in a blanket clause to cover things like "Any worn part encountered during repairs". If such a clause is given then clarification should be given as to what parts might be worn, and if encountered, what additional costs would be expected. In this manner a maximum cost can be anticipated. If not taken into account, exclusions may turn the lowest quote into the highest bill.

ASSESSING QUOTATIONS

Quotations can only be compared if they are based on the same requirements. Sometimes, the requirements are not obvious and restorers will each come up with different proposals and suggestions. The customer might have to go back and ask for more information or clarifications. Churches should seek the help of their Diocesan Clocks Adviser to help assess quotations, or a specialist in the case of Heritage Organisations.

There are many factors that will affect which restorer is chosen to carry out the work.
  The price
  The conservator / restorer, their approach, attitude and experience
  The work proposed (some work eg on dials, might need several people)

If quotations and proposals vary widely, then additional quotations should be sought.

Before placing an order, make sure the price quoted is the price you will pay, or if there are exclusions you understand what they are.

A good way to help assess the most appropriate restorer for the job is to visit their workshop and talk to some of their recent customers.

WARRANTIES

Warranties must be taken into account when comparing quotations. Look at the economics of a job and these warranties fall into two camps: Repair work and equipment supplied.

Repair work should be guaranteed for at least a year.

Today domestic electronics and white goods are often supplied with warranties that cover perhaps 3 years. A warranty on a new car might be as much as 5 years. For automatic winders, night silencers, auto correctors and electro hammers it would be not unreasonable to expect warranties of 5 to 10 years.

When a clock has been giving a lot of problems, or is worn, a restoration is needed. This would probably entail the removal of the clock. The sort of work needed is likely to be re-bushing of worn holes, repair or replacement of an escape wheel, fitting of new weight lines and of course, cleaning. Make sure that any building work needed is carried out whilst the clock is out and the clock room cleaned in readiness for the clock's return.

Dials and motionworks

Working on dials needs special steeplejack-like skills to approach the dial. Moving a large cast-iron dial needs careful attention and probably a crane. Even a four feet diameter copper dial becomes difficult to handle when it is up a tower exposed to the wind.

Dials too may need painting and restoration; in a large overhaul, work on dials and motion work may account for half the bill. Dials are the part seen by the public and for that reason they should be restored with sensitivity in their appropriate style and materials.

Anyone chosen to do dial restoration must be skilled in this particular aspect of turret clock work.

Installing Automatic Winders

The Church Buildings Council (CBC) has a policy on how automatic winders should be installed. See the CBC web site for detailed information.

Auto-winding should normally be applied to the barrel arbor

In exceptional circumstances, and where this can be demonstrated to be for the benefit of the clock, auto-winding may be applied to the 2nd arbor, but never any higher in the train

Winding jacks are never to be used as part of an auto-winding installation

The clock must always remain completely intact and the installation be capable of removal so that it can be returned to manual winding.

Moving Turret Clocks

Moving the position of a turret clock in a secular building is rarely needed, but in churches the need sometime arises when bells have been rehung or augmented. Every effort should be made to keep the clock in the position in which it was first installed, and that moving a clock should only be considered in extremes after all other options have been fully investigated and discounted.

The Diocesan Clocks and Bells Advisers must be involved at a very early stage so that they can work together to ensure that a possible relocation is properly investigated before any faculty application is made. This will avoid any conflict of interest taking place between the requirements of the clock and bell.

Replacing the clock with an electric motor to make more space for bell augmentation or rehanging in a new frame is not acceptable.

The new location for the clock and associated lead-off work should allow safe easy access and not create cramped or difficult working conditions for winding or servicing. The position chosen should be strong enough to support the weight of the clock and its weights. The lead-off work and bell wire need direct routes to the dial and bell with the minimum of changes in direction. If hand-wound, sufficient fall for the weights is required so that the clock lasts a week between windings; electric auto-winding is often fitted when the clock is relocated.

Provision should be made to contain safely the weights if the lines break or the pendulum if its suspension spring fails.

Every effort should be made to retain earlier weight chutes, and if auto-winding is installed, a secure place must be found for old weights, pulleys and winding handle no longer currently in use and all labelled clearly for identification.

Illuminated dials

Illuminated dials were traditionally made of a skeleton of cast iron and glazed with opal glass. Illumination on the inside was initially by gas and this was soon replaced by electricity in the 20th century. Incandesant bulbs were replaced by fluorescent tubes and today a wide range of luminaires are available from conventional low-energy bulbs to LED lights. LED lights offer small size thus making them easy to install where motionworks and counterbalances make things difficult. Low power and long lifetimes are other benefits. LED can be run off low voltages and this can be a great advantage in damp environments.

In new clock installations hands can be illuminated with LED strip lights

Adding quarter striking and tune playing

It is now an easy matter to expand facilities on a turret clock by adding quarter striking to an hour striking movement, or by adding both hour and quarter-striking to a timepiece. Electro hammers and some electronics to provide the sequence of notes can be installed without altering the clock. It might seem attractive to have an electronic master clock to control the striking. Far better and less cost, is to add a switch on the movement that will initiate the striking. In this manner the striking is always in step with the time indicated on the dial and not early or late with respect to the mechanical clock.

Similarly a tune player can be started so that it follows the hour striking.

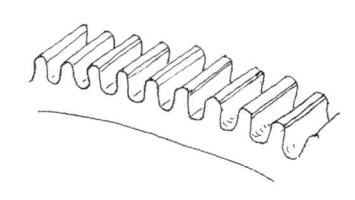

WHO WILL DO THE WORK REQUIRED?

People who work on turret clocks can range from a local clockmaker who occasionally works on turret clocks, through to individuals who are employed full-time in the trade to smaller companies that are able to carry out any work anywhere in the country to large companies that can undertake international projects. There is a place for all these clockmakers and choosing the most appropriate one is important. Where possible use a qualified professional who is engaged full-time in turret clock work.

Finding and choosing a turret clock restorer

A competent person should carry out any service or repair work. The best qualification is someone who is experienced in turret clock work and who has a catalogue of successful work with satisfied customers that are willing to give references. There is no formal horological qualification available for those who work specifically on turret clocks, but you should expect to see MBHI or FBHI after the name of the person you are dealing with.

The approach to the work required

The view of those commissioning work might range from one of 'The lowest cost is the best' to 'The clock is unique and must be fixed, it costs what it costs'. In reality most people are proud of their clock, its heritage and its place in the local community. The important thing is to impart your love of the clock to potential restorers, and communicate to them that a quality job is required. Be aware that the lowest price tender can end up as the most expensive unless all aspects of the work have been covered. There have been cases where additional money was asked by the restorer for fixing problems that they did not spot or where complete areas were omitted e.g. the bell hammers and wires.

Qualifications

The British Horological Institute (BHI) maintains a list of their members who are qualified to BHI standards and who are obliged to follow the BHI code of practice. The BHI will provide names of restorers in your area; make sure to ask for someone experienced in turret clock work. Repairers can be searched for on the BHI web site.

BHI member grades are as follows…

    MBHI   Member BHI. A qualified member.
    FBHI   Fellow BHI. A qualified member with extensive proven experience.

The grades CMBHI, LBHI and GradBHI are no longer in operation.

The Professional Accreditation of Conservator-Restorers (PACR) is an assessment scheme owned by the Institute of Conservation (ICON). PACR enables qualified and experienced practitioners in all conservation disciplines to achieve Accredited Conservator-Restorer (ACR) status; essential for inclusion in the Conservation Register. Turret clock restoration is a discipline that is relatively new to formal conservation techniques so the ICON web site lists only a few persons who do turret clock work.

There are individuals or companies in the UK that deal regularly with turret clocks. Each one has a particular approach and there is room for the one-man-operator, through the small company to the large organization. There are six main features of a good restorer:

1 They have a passion for the historical and technical side of turret clocks
2 They have a record of satisfied customers
3 They provide good value.
4 They are technically competent.
5 They have a well-equipped workshop in which they do their work.
6 They operate good business practices and carry the appropriate insurance.

Turret clock restorers might advertise in such publications as Yellow pages, Diocesan newspapers and directories and The Ringing World. A search of the internet will also be useful. One of the best plans is to ask around for the experience of other local churches, schools and town halls that have clocks. A good recommendation is one of the best adverts a restorer can have.

OTHER ISSUES

Replacing a Mechanical Turret Clock

One argument for replacing a mechanical clock with an electronic one is the belief that such an installation once fitted can be forgotten. This is not so, maintenance will still be needed. The motionwork behind the dial will need annual cleaning and lubrication. A dial will need periodic painting and gilding.

It may seem at first glance that installing a new electronic clock is cheaper than having work done on a mechanical clock. Electronic equipment has a finite life and when a component fails causing the clock to stop there are two options. Module replacement is a common technique, but with components and systems going obsolete a common solution is the complete replacement of the electronic clock system. Like a TV, burglar alarm or a computer printer, repair to component level is rarely an economic option.

Doing a lifetime cost assessment is worthwhile. Estimates will have to be made but a 10 year lifetime on an electronic system is reasonable comparing it with domestic equipment. Servicing to the motionworks will still be needed and since most electronics has rechargeable batteries then these might need replacement during the equipment's life.

For the mechanical clock annual servicing will be needed and any restoration or automatic winding costs would have to be accounted for. The lifetime of a good automatic winder is about 20 years.

Retiring a Mechanical Turret Clock

Retiring a church clock is very rare, but clock retirement is more common in secular buildings. For both church and other buildings, particularly those that are listed, the correct procedures must be followed to make sure that the removal is legitimate.

Suppose a community building such as a hospital has been demolished; finding a suitable home for the clock should be carefully considered.

If it was decided to place the retired clock in a museum, then one that is registered under the Museum Accreditation Scheme is the best choice. This ensures that the chosen museum follows proper practices dealing with artefacts in every aspect from acquisition to storage, through cataloguing, display and proper public access. An accredited museum will have an acquisition and disposal policy document stating how materials will be dispersed in the event of no longer being required or due to closure. Anyone considering putting a clock in a museum should investigate this and be sure of the long-term arrangements that are promised. A privately-owned museum, particularly a specialist one, might seem a good choice, but these can be broken up when the owner dies, retires or changes their collecting whim.

Museums do not display everything they have; often about 80% of their collection is kept in store rooms. A donor must clearly understand whether their turret clock will be put on display or not. Museums are not secure depositories of artefacts. Public museums are not immune to problems as local authority and central government change policies.

Depositing an artefact in a museum must be accompanied by a proper legal agreement. Examples are that the clock is given to the museum as a donation, or the clock is on loan to the museum for a defined period, say perhaps 10 years. There is no such situation as a 'Permanent loan' Once the title of ownership changes the clock is no longer the property of the donor and they have no further control over the clock. Say a public library was demolished and its turret clock given to a museum. In the future a 'Friends of the Library' group might want to reinstate the turret clock in some way in a new building. They would have no legal right over the clock and could not demand its return.

Where a turret clock is loaned to a museum then certain legal criteria have to be agreed between the lender and the museum. Insurance is one, others might include cleaning, maintenance and display.

A turret clock preserved in a museum may be run as a working exhibit. The museum would need to make sure the display is safe, eg no one can walk under the weights or be hit by a rotating fly.

LIFETIME COSTS

At the first sight, replacing a mechanical clock with an electrical one might seem financially to be a good idea. Domestic electronics like a TV have a life time of say 5 years, consumer goods like a washing machine perhaps 10 years would be a good life. Industrial electronics are more likely to be 10 years and industrial electrical equipment say 20 years.

It would be wise to conside the whole life costs of a project involving the replacing of a mechanical clock with an electronic solution. This involves making estimates of how long an item will last and what the likely service costs might be. The following figures can only be starting points, but are based on the experience of those involved with turret clocks.

Item	Lifetime
Basic synchronous motor	20 - 30 years
Electrical automatic winder	25 - 50 years
DC motor with brushes	10 - 15 years
Sealed rechargeable battery	4 - 5 years
Electro hammer	10 - 20 years
Electronic master clocks	10 -15 years
Any unit containing electronics	10 - 15 years
Annual service	Required for all clocks with mechanical dials
Warranties	5 to 10 years expected

Doing the comparisons may be difficult, but look at the cost per year for all the alternatives. Remember that at the end of a cycle a mechanical clock is still there.

THE FUTURE FOR RETIRED CLOCKS IN CHURCH OF ENGLAND BUILDINGS

In the event of a clock being retired with the agreement of all concerned and the diocese a suitable home for it should be found. Generally the best place is to leave the clock where it is, up a tower. Churches sometimes put old clocks on display in a suitable part of the nave. A clock as an occasionally-working exhibit generates public interest and is good form of preservation. The downside of this can be that what starts as a proud exhibit cared for by the parishioners can end up as an uncared for dusty piece of machinery and a nuisance to succeeding parishioners. The clock is then at greater long-term risk. A faculty is always needed to remove a clock.

Weights, Chutes and Pulleys

When automatic winders are fitted to church clocks this is sometimes part of other schemes. These might require the removal of internal wooden weight chutes to make more room.

Where possible weight chutes should be retained. Pulleys and weights should be retained and stored somewhere appropriate; e.g. out of the way in the bottom of the weight chute or in the clock case. The redundant winding handle should be stored in the clock case.

Old electrical clocks

There are some electrical impulse clocks driven by master clocks that date from 1910 and after. The first synchronous motors were employed in the 1930s. Electrical installations of this age can still operate in a satisfactory manner. However they require specialist knowledge from the restorer, and are getting to an age when synchronous motors are worn out or the safety of electrical equipment might be questioned. The Antiquarian Horological Society has a specialist Electrical Horology Group that has members knowledgeable in diverse aspects of electrical horology.

Church of England Faculties & DAC Advisers

The Church of England has a control system, the Faculty Jurisdiction, that is roughly equivalent to secular planning law, though control extends to a greater level of detail than with a secular building. Any work to a church clock, other than maintenance, basic repairs, or replacement of wire lines, auto-winder motors and switches, requires a faculty. Faculties are granted by the Chancellor of the diocese (a legal officer) who is advised by the Diocesan Advisory Committee (DAC). Most dioceses have a specialist clocks adviser, who advises the Diocesan Advisory Committee. The adviser is available to help parishes, and discuss proposed work with the clock restorer. There is a Forum in which the various clocks advisers are able to communicate with each other and to discuss issues.

No work should commence until a faculty has been granted. Faculty Jurisdiction applies to all contents of a church, even if the ownership of the item lies elsewhere. Sometimes clocks were purchased by public subscription and are the property of a local council; the Faculty Jurisdiction still applies where the local council owns the clock in the church.

Publicity

Where a clock is in good condition, there are opportunities for a clock-related project, and indeed one which could be fulfilled on a low budget. What about producing a booklet on the clock? This could, of course, be combined with a restoration project and could even be a simple display panel at the tower with good quality photos and some text. Bodies giving grants are likely to pay for this as part of the clock restoration. If the clock is strongly associated with a person is there a photo of them, are they alive or still remembered? Old buildings usually have a printed guide of some sort, this could be updated to include details of the clock. Some places have produced leaflets or booklets on the clock itself, or the clock, tower and bells. Such a booklet gives equal scope to the historian and researcher, clock winder, photographer, desk top publisher, artist and so on. What might at first sight be an apparently dry subject of interest to a few technical specialists, can be brought to life to catch the imagination of those in the locality as well as passing visitors. Consider the original reason for the clock's installation, the minutes in record books, old quotations, bills and correspondence from the maker, newspaper articles over the years and so on. Often the clock case has comments scribbled in its odd corners recording such events as a new clock winder, the death of the King, outbreak of war, a dial repainted or repairs to clock. The winder too is living history and is bound to have some information and anecdotes about their charge. Once written, sketched, photographed and put into a word processor or desk-top-publisher, it remains to be printed. With today's print on demand facility booklets can be produced in small quantities at reasonable price.

Fund Raising

When engaging in a major project concering a clock it is wise to form a dedicated Clock Restoration Committee at an early stage. There are many sources of grant funding-- it is a case of finding them. Heritage Lottery is one and the Church Buildings Council can award grants for clock work.

Local charities should be explored and local councillors often have a discretionary sum they can award for deserving projects.

To raise money for a dial restoration one church had a 'Sponsor a numeral' fund raising event where people could 'buy' a minute mark or a Roman numeral. There is the old variation on raffle tickets where a wind-up clock is fully wound and sealed in a box. Contributors then guess when the clock will stop and the winner is found when the box is opened. Dial floodlighting, where it exists, could be a means of sponsorship. People might want to pay for the illumination on a certain day in memory of an event personal to them. Holding a concert or service on the theme of time is another scheme.

Health & Safety

The profile of health & safety issues has expanded rapidly over past years and this has now had an impact on the world of turret clocks. In the main visiting and winding a turret clock presents much the same risk as crossing a road. However, it is essential that the risks involved are clearly understood and catered for by the clock owner and anyone attending or winding the clock. From time to time one is told "It's not safe up there, only the clock winder is allowed up the tower". If it's not safe for a sensible informed visitor then it is not safe for the clock winder. Such a statement cannot absolve the clock owner from liability.

Health and safety is all about being sensible and not taking unnecessary risks. It is important that the clock carries on being wound and looked after in a proper manner. Where health and safety issues are identified look for solutions rather than locking the tower and putting up a Keep Out notice.

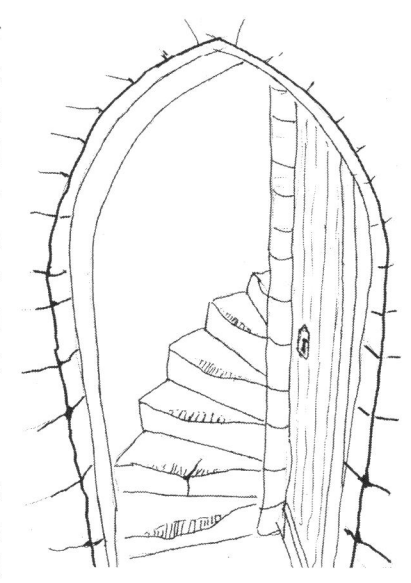

How safe is the access?

Safety in Visiting a Clock for Winding

Some simple procedures can be employed to ensure that should something go wrong whilst winding or visiting a clock then suitable help can be summoned. Many churches and heritage buildings will demand lone working procedures. Such a procedure would possibly include such systems as:

Two people working together at all times

One person on their own needs to notify a nominated person that they are visiting the clock and on completion of the job they notify the same person they are out of the building. If the person working on the clock has not contacted the nominated person within a specified time, then a search is instigated.

A mobile phone is carried.

Notices such as 'Worker in Tower' are displayed.

Locked In Strategy

Anyone working regularly on turret clocks is likely to experience being locked in a tower at some time. Such an incident can arise from the key holder thinking the building was empty and locking up, someone inadvertently locking a door that they thought had been left open, or from a malicious act. Anticipating such a situation is being pre armed.

Avoidance of being locked in is certainly the best policy making sure that people are aware that someone is working on the clock, locking padlocks so they cannot be snapped shut and having 'Worker in Tower' notices.

Strategies to cope with the locked-in situation could involve:
Operating a lone working plan like that above

Keep keys and padlocks with you
Carrying a mobile phone
Having a whistle or personal alarm to attract attention
Knowing how to release the striking train so the clock will continuously ring a bell and attract attention.

Very often clocks have to be accessed by a platform and these do not always have a suitable handrail, so stepping backwards and falling is a possibility. Fitting a wooden or steel tubular hand rail solves the problem.

Handrails can be built round an unprotected platrform

Risk Assessment Check Sheets

The following check lists are supplied as a guide, so churches, heritage buildings and public buildings can have a starting point for considering health & safety issues. Some are very specific to turret clocks and some are general in nature. These lists are not claimed to be exhaustive and to cover every situation, but they should provide a good starting point where no risk assessment has taken place. Guidance on risk assessment is also available from insurers.

It might seem tedious, but those responsible for clocks should carry out some appropriate level of risk assessment. This should be written up, signed, dated and placed on file. It is hoped that it will never be needed, but in today's society where it is becoming the norm to look for someone to blame and to sue, a risk assessment may be useful to demonstrate that a proper evaluation had been carried out.

Check lists are provided of hazards that may be experienced. This 'check list' is divided into the principal areas that concern a turret clock. These lists may not be exhaustive, so extra items may be included if necessary. Some things like checking of electrical installations, fire extinguishers and lightning conductors are included for completeness, but are normally the responsibility of those who care for the building.

Professional risk assessment often involves estimating the possibility of an event happening along with the severity of its result. The lists that follow make no attempt to go to that level, they are only intended to highlight some common issues.

Turret Clock Health & Safety Survey Check Sheet Topics

General Details
Location
Date of Survey
Survey Carried out by
Signed
Dated
For all possible listed hazards enter Safe or unsafe and enter a comment.

General Safety Issues
Does the building have a lightning conductor?
Has a survey been carried out for asbestos?
Have the electrics been tested, including all electrics up the tower?
Are there adequate and appropriate fire extinguishers in the tower?
Is there a first aid kit available?
Can people be locked in by accident or malicious act?
Is there a procedure by which a clock winder who is locked in can summon help?

Access Checklist
This refers to access to the clock as reasonably needed by the clock winder, or persons going to make adjustments to the clock.

Is there adequate lighting?
Are stone steps in good condition?
Is there a hand rope / rail?
Are wooden ladders in good condition with no missing or damaged rungs?
Do vertical ladders present a hazard?
Are all ladders secured so they cannot slip?
Do trap doors have a means to prevent falling on a head?
Is the flooring free of decay and holes or wormed flooring?
Have holes for weights been protected so no one inadvertently falls down?
If there is a raised platform for the clock, does it have adequate rails or protection?
Is the tower free from bird droppings & nesting materials?

Weight Lines
Many clocks are driven by weights that range from around 50lbs to as much as half a ton. The weight lines are made of steel wire, though sometimes rope is encountered. The free end of the line is attached to the top of the weight shaft, often by screw eyes or U bolts. Often weights are enclosed in a shaft, but not always.

Weight Lines Checklist
    Are steel lines free from rust?
    Are steel lines free from being polished smooth?
    Steel lines free from prickles?
    Lines more than 20 years old?
    Doubtful line attachment in roof, eg just a knot?
    Doubtful line attachment on barrel e.g. line runs out and line held by a nail?
    Wormed / rotten supporting beams?
    Unknown condition of screwed-in eyes?
    Rusty lines particularly near attachments?
    Line attachment points inaccessible?
    Fibre ropes in poor condition?
    Pulleys of sufficient diameter to avoid straining line? This is particularly important with small lines on automatic winders. A 5 inch pulley is generally an adequate size.

Weights

The reality is that over the last 200 years the number of fatalities directly due to a turret clock is still in single figures. Excluded from this number are secondary causes such as heart attacks and falls whist climbing church towers.

Falling weights due to line breakage cause significant damage. In falling a weight could cause other weights to follow, it could break out of the weight chute, go through floors and injure people nearby.

Some clock installations have a box of sand or broken bricks at the bottom of the weight shaft to absorb the energy of a falling weight. However, weights do not always fall straight.

Weights Checklist
    Centre stem not rusted?
    Weight cheeses that cannot fall off?
    Public not able to walk underneath weights?
    Access for clockmaker to bottom of weight shaft?
    In the event of a line failure, what would happen to the weights?
    Bottom of weight cupboard not used for storage, electricity consumer units etc?

Dials

Many dials were installed in the Victorian era and now their fixings are corroded. Inspection really needs access by scaffolding or a steeplejack. However, some idea may be gained by inspection with binoculars or telescope.

Note: If scaffolding is up the tower, get a turret clockmaker to remove the hands and service the motionwork. Don't ask them to do this the day before the scaffolding is to be taken down!

Inaccessible dials are normally approached by trained persons who use abseiling techniques.

Dials Checklist

The following items have been viewed through binoculars judged as best as can be ascertained.

No broken glass in illuminated dials.
Fixing bolts and staples secure.
Fixing bolts in sound wood or stonework.
No broken glass in illuminated dials.
No cracks in cast-iron dials.

Bells and Hammers

The bell hammers are definitely part of a clock installation. So often these are forgotten and in poor states. Faulty hammers can cause much damage to a swinging bell and its wheel.

Bell Hammers Checklist

Fixing of hammers and cranks secure?
Check springs correctly adjusted so hammer head just clear of bell?
Ringers' clock hammer pull-offs operate correctly?

Others Checklist

Are there any other areas of risk that have been identified. In particular, are there any that mean stopping the clock until it is made safe or that no one should go up the tower until something is repaired?

MOBILE PHONE TRANSMITTERS

A new hazard is the mobile phone transmitter. These transmitters are being installed increasingly in clock towers that offer space for equipment and a good height for aerials. Churches often welcome these since they provide a good source of income. Radiation from transmitting aerials is a hazard and one that cannot be seen. There should be no appreciable radiation inside the tower that would affect those inside. If a dial had to be accessed from outside by a restorer then checking with the transmitter operator and building authorities would be essential before work is commenced.

Phone installations take up quite a lot of space; the clockmaker should be consulted before a transmitter is installed to make sure that the installation does not interfere with the clock. Heat generated by the installation might mean the clock needs more frequent lubrication.

MERCURY IN TURRET CLOCKS

Mercury is a liquid metal that can be particularly dangerous in vapour form and in its various compounds. Reduction of Hazardous Substances (RoHS) is a European directive that applies to electrical and electronic equipment made after 1st July 2006 and bans the use of mercury, and other named toxic chemicals. Pre-2006 equipment is excluded from the directive.

Mercury can be encountered in turret clocks in electrical switches. These comprise a glass tube that has two contacts; a small quantity of mercury is enclosed in the sealed tube and when the tube is tilted contact is made or broken. In turret clocks mercury switches are almost always inside a case protecting them from accidental damage.

The sealed glass mercury switch presents no hazards in normal use and there is no reason to remove switches on a health & safety or RoHS basis. If the switch has been damaged it can be replaced since this is a service operation. Mercury switches are very difficult to source so a mechanical switch might well have to be used instead.

The second type of switch sometimes encountered is a high-current switch that was used for dial lighting. The switch comprises two open pots partially filled with mercury. A pivoted arm activated by a solenoid has two fingers on the end that dip into the two pots completing the circuit. When the fingers are withdrawn, the circuit is broken. This type of switch is particularly dangerous since mercury vapour can be produced when the contact is made or broken. However, it is highly unlikely that these switches are still being used in clock towers. If one is discovered it should be checked to make sure the mercury has been removed. If some remains it is advisable to remove it using a plastic syringe and to dispose of it in a proper manner.

The following notes are for a guide only. If a small quantity of mercury has been spilt, say due to a broken switch, it can be dealt with as follows. Ensure adequate ventilation and wear rubber gloves. Using a piece of card or brush carefully move the globules of mercury until they join together into one big globule. This can then be sucked up using a small plastic syringe or bulb pipette and the collected mercury stored in a plastic bottle. Do NOT use a vacuum cleaner since this will generate mercury vapour. Consult your local authority for proper disposal procedures. Commercially produced mercury spillage kits are available.

COLLECTING TURRET CLOCKS

COLLECTING PHILOSOPHY

People collect all sorts of things from stamps to steam engines and some people collect turret clocks. Often these are clock collectors who want to have one turret clock as part of a wider collection. Here a small domestic sized clock is preferable that fits into an alcove or hallway. Some collectors are more serious and use a garage or a barn that soon fills up. Turret clock dials can indeed be incorporated into buildings; garages and stables are the most popular.

POINTS TO CONSIDER

A small turret clock with a seconds length pendulum is highly suitable for incorporation into a domestic environment or the gable end of a garage. A clock that is complete with pendulum, dial, hands, motionworks, weights, pulleys, winding handle, bell and bell hammer commands a high price compared to a movement on its own. When buying be sure as to exactly what comes with a movement. Clocks offered for sale are very often just a movement even lacking the pendulum and weights.

Most turret clocks tend to have long pendulums, either 1¼ seconds (length 5 feet) 1½ seconds (length 9 feet) or 2 seconds (length 14 feet). Clocks with longer pendulums are less desirable and more difficult to install as a going exhibit.

Going period is another issue. The small clock quoted with probably run for a day with a weight drop of 3 feet, but larger clocks with longer pendulums need heavier weights and might need longer drops to accommodate a day's running. Restricted drop can be overcome by employing a heavier weight on multiple pulleys. However, multiple pulleys are inefficient and very large weights are generally not suitable in a domestic setting. Of course, the addition of an automatic winder will remove these restrictions.

ACQUIRING A CLOCK & PROVENANCE

With turret clocks, there are ethical considerations to be borne in mind. Turret clocks may be bought in auctions both local and on-line, or privately from another collector. It is important to have the confidence to know that the clock has been legally removed from a building. With the demolition of Victorian factories and public buildings there has been a wealth of clocks coming on to the market. Clocks also appear as buildings are modernised and mechanical movements fall prey to cold economics, discarded in favour of an electronic solution.

If offered a clock from a C of E church then be suspicious and do make sure that a faculty has been granted for its removal. If in doubt contact the diocese. Canon (Church) law, like other legislation, is passed by Parliament and as such carries enforceable penalties. Best to check first than to be held responsible for its return. Similarly a clock from a listed or heritage building might also be subject to restrictions as to its disposal.

Knowing the provenance of a clock not only adds to the clock's history, but also enhances its value. It also makes it easier to pass on when the time comes to sell the clock as the buyer has the assurance that the clock was legally procured. So, do try to find out where a clock came from, and do document everything you uncover.

RESTORATION

It is a great temptation to the collector on acquiring a new turret clock to immediately start restoring the movement. Polishing of brasswork and repainting are often the order of the day. Sadly the colour chosen is often the colour of their front door; the half full tin of paint in the garage being hastily utilised.

Now collectors of antiques usually like their antiques looking old, keeping the patina, but clean and usable. The new turret clock collector is strongly advised to look at their clock for a long time before engaging on any major work.

DISPOSAL

When the time comes to sell a turret clock the options are by auction or through friends and contacts. Other possibilities are return it to the building from whence it came or into a museum in that locality. See the earlier notes on the disposal of clocks into museums.

A cast-iron 4' 6" dial as a feature on the garden shed of a collector

Turret Clock Recording

The Turret Clock Group of the Antiquarian Horological Society has a project to record and document as many turret clocks as possible in the UK. A two-page recording form is included in this booklet and you may make copies of this form as required.

Do not be put off by the form's apparent complexity, at the very least try to record the items in the boxes outlined with a bold line. Please help by recording any turret clocks you see. In the fullness of time, records will be available on computer disk and in hard copy for researchers to study. An incomplete record is better than no record at all.

Describing a Turret Clock

Turret clocks may be simply described by the number of trains, the type of frame and the escapement. Thus the clock at Westminster is a three train flatbed with gravity escapement.

Try to record the items in the boxes outlined with a bold line. Please help by recording any turret clocks you see.

The database is in the process of being made accessible on the net, do a search to find the lastest status.

'Excellent' describes a clock which is exceptionally clean, well-maintained and everything works.

'Good' describes a clock which is clean and everything works

'Fair' describes a clock which is running, has no major problems, but is rather greasy or oily.

'Poor' describes a clock which is running, or able to run, but is in a very dirty condition.

'Derelict' describes a clock which cannot run, is dirty, rusty and may have had parts removed and lost.

When complete, please return this form to the address at the end of this form. Visit the AHS web site, the database for viewing and adding records is in the process of being implemented.

PROJECT 2000
TURRET CLOCK RECORDING FORM FOR CLOCKS IN THE UK
Antiquarian Horological Society
Turret Clock Group

Sadly, as buildings vanish, or economic pressures mount, turret clocks are being lost. By recording what exists now we hope to do two things: Provide a store of information for future generations and to foster a wider understanding and appreciation of turret clocks. In this way, more clocks will be preserved as knowledge grows. A survey of as many turret clocks in the British Isles as possible is being made, information is stored on a computer database and will be made available from time to time. By completing this form you are contributing to preserving turret clocks.

Please complete as much of this form as possible, circle the appropriate code in each section. To help you complete this form see the 'The Turret Clock Keeper's Handbook' available from the AHS. At the least, please try to complete all the basic information on the first page.
If you are able to supply a photograph of the clock, mark the back with the location of the clock, your name and the date

When complete, please return this form to the address on the back of this form.

Location			
Name of Town / Village / Area of City			
Name of City if Applicable			
County			
Name of Building, Dedication (if church)			
Address			
Location of clock in building e.g. tower, nave.			
Grid Ref if possible eg TL 042670			
Previous Location if moved from another building / place.			
Photo attached to this report?	YES		NO
Guide / literature with this report?	YES		NO

Comments; including any historical information about the clock, sundials, other horological items.

Tick if location of clock to be kept confidential, e.g. collections and private houses...................... ☐

TURRET CLOCK DETAILS

Maker(s)		
Maker (s) Surnames(s		name
Maker 1st names(s)		fnam
Maker's Town		town
Date on clock		date
or - Date circa		cdate
Setting dial or nameplate Inscription		setd

© AHS 2005. Permission to photocopy granted   Page 1 of 2

Frames types	
End to end Birdcage	EE
Side by side Birdcage	BC
Posted	FP
Double-framed	DF
Plate and Spacer	PS
Flat Bed	FB
A-Frame	AF
Other (Specify)	

Size of Frame	
Length in ins	
Height in ins	
Depth in ins	

Frame Material	
Wrought Iron	WI
Cast Iron	CI
Brass	BR
Wood	WO
Other (Specify)	

Trains & Going Period	
Going	1T
Going & Striking	2T
Going & Striking & Chiming	3T
Number of wheels in going train	
Number of wheels in striking train	

Trains Contd	
Number of wheels in chiming train	
Strike control rack or count wheel	
Tune barrel (Carillon)	CR
Automata	AU
Other (Specify)	
1 Day going period	1D
8 Day going period	8D
Other (Specify)	

Escapement	
Recoil	RC
Deadbeat	DB
Pinwheel	PW
Double Three-legged Gravity	DT
Verge & Foliot	VF
Verge & Short bob pendulum	VP
Compensation pendulum	CP
Other (Specify)	
Length of pendulum (ft) or	
Pendulum period in seconds	

Misc	
Winding jack	JA
Other (Specify)	

Electrical clocks	
Waiting Train	WT
Synchronous Motor	SY
Impulse	IM
Other (Specify)	

Autowinders	
Huygens endless chain.	HY
Monkey up the rope	MR
Differential	DR
Power winder	PW
Other / Manufacturer (Specify)	

Dials	
Number of dials	ND
Wood	WO
Stone	ST
Cast iron	CI
Copper	CO
Lead	LD
1 Hand	1H
2 Hands	2H
Other (Specify)	

Condition of clock	
Excellent	EX
Good	GD
Fair	FR
Poor	PR
Derelict	DT

Recorder Information	
Name	
Code Letters of recorder if known	
Address of recorder if not a regular contributor Tel	
Date of Survey	

I am not member of the AHS and would like information on Project 2000 when it is published........... ☐

Please send me .... more survey forms

To conserve funds, we do not normally acknowledge receipt of recording forms. If you would like an acknowledgement of receipt tick here............. ☐

Thank you for your support

Serial Number given by Database Manager	

Please return this form to...
The Turret Clock Database Manager
Antiquarian Horological Society
4 Lovat Lane
London EC3R 8DT

Glossary of Terms

AHS	Antiquarian Horological Society.
Arbor	Horological term for axle.
Arm chair	Incorrect term for double framed.
Automatic winder	Electrically powered device to wind clock.
Barrel	Wood or metal cylinder around which the weight line is wound.
Bell crank	Lever to transfer the pull of a wire through 90°.
Belfry	Chamber where bells are hung.
Bell hammer	Hammer to sound bell.
Bevel gear	Set of gears to transfer turning of a rod through 90°.
BHI	British Horological Institute.
Birdcage	Type of clock frame. (End to end or side by side.)
Bob	Weight on the end of the pendulum.
Bolt and Shutter	Type of maintaining power.
Bushing	Brass bearing in which pivots run.
Cam	Shaped device to raise a lever.
Carillon	Common description of a tune barrel. Set of 23 or more bells.
Cast iron	Iron cast in a mould.
CBC	The Church Buildings Council.
Centre wheel	Wheel in going train turning once an hour.
Chair frame	Incorrect term for double framed.
Chiming	The sounding of bells each quarter of an hour.
Click	Device to stop a wheel turning backwards.
Compensation pendulum	Pendulum specially constructed so that it keeps correct time at different temperatures.
Count wheel	Wheel to set the number of blows struck when the clock strikes.
Crutch	Device which connects the escapement to the pendulum.
Dead beat	Type of escapement.
Differential (Epicyclic)	Gears used in a maintaining power or automatic winder.
Diocesan clocks adviser	Person familiar with turret clocks who helps local diocese.
Dog clutch	Device to set hands to time.
Double framed	Type of turret clock frame.
Double three-legged gravity	Type of escapement.
Electro hammer	An electrically operated bell hammer
End to end	Type of train arrangement in a birdcage frame.
Epicyclic	Gears used in a maintaining power or automatic winder.
Escape wheel	Wheel on which the pallets act.
Escapement	Device to release one tooth at a time and to impulse pendulum.
Face	Incorrect term for a dial.
Faculty	Legal document in the C of E giving a parish permission to do specified work on a church building or its fittings.
Flatbed	Type of turret clock frame.
Fly	Fan-shaped device to limit the speed of striking.
Foliot	Timekeeping device consisting of a weighted bar.

Frame	Iron, wood or brass structure to contain movement's wheels.
Friction clutch	Device to set hands to time.
Going train	Train of gears which drive the dial.
Great wheel	The largest wheel in a clock train.
Harrison's	Type of maintaining power.
Huygens endless chain	An endless chain used in an automatic winder.
Impulse movement	Electrical movement which advances hands in half minute steps.
Jack	Decorative figure or automata which strikes a bell.
Leading off rod	Rod connecting the clock to a dial.
Leading off work	Collection of rods and gears to connect the clock to a dial.
Line	Line suspending the driving weight, usually of galvanised steel.
Maintaining power	Device to keep clock running whilst it is being wound.
Monkey up the rope	Automatic winder where the motor climbs up a chain.
Motion work	Reduction gears behind a dial to drive the hour hand from the minute hand.
Movement	Clock mechanism.
Night silencing	Device to turn off striking and chiming during night hours.
Override switch	Safety switch on an automatic winder.
Pallets	Parts of an escapement which engage the escape wheel teeth.
Pendulum	Device swinging at a constant rate.
Pinion	Small gear of 12 teeth or less.
Pinwheel	Type of escapement.
Pivot	Part about which a wheel turns.
Plate and spacer	Type of clock frame.
Posted frame	Type of clock frame.
Power winder	Automatic winder which winds up original weights.
Pulley	Used to guide weight lines.
Quarter striking	Chimes which sound every 15 minutes.
Rack	Device to count number of blows to be sounded at the hour.
Ratchet	Gear wheel with saw-like teeth arrested by a click.
Rating nut	Nut to adjust the timekeeping of a pendulum.
Recoil	Type of escapement.
Setting dial	Internal dial to enable external dial to be set to time.
Side by Side	Type of train arrangement in a birdcage frame.
Snail	Cam which sets how far a rack falls.
Striking	The sounding of a bell at the hour.
Suspension spring	Thin spring from which the pendulum hangs.
Synchronous motor	Electrical motor driven by the mains.
Timepiece	A clock that only shows the time
Ting Tang	Quarter striking sounded on two bells of different notes.
Train	Collection of gear wheels.
Tune barrel	Device to play tunes on bells.
Turret clock	Clock with a public dial and/or sounding on a bell.
Up	Bells supported mouth up and ready to ring.

Verge	Type of escapement.
Waiting train	Type of electrical turret clock.
Warning	The release of the striking or a chiming train a few minutes. before striking or chiming.
Winding crank	Handle to wind clock.
Winding jack	Reduction gear to make winding a clock easier.
Winding square	Square on barrel onto which the winding crank is fitted.
Wrought iron	Iron forged to shape by a blacksmith.

Turret Clock Sources of Information

Antiquarian Horological Society (AHS)

The AHS is a learned body dedicated to the widening and dissemination of historical horological knowledge. It publishes a quarterly journal, books and has a library. There is a specialist Turret Clock Group and also an Electrical Horology Group. The Turret Clock Group may be able to give advice on the historical aspect of turret clocks.

Antiquarian Horological Society
New House
Ticehurst
East Sussex
TN5 7AL
01580 200155
email secretary@ahsoc.demon.co.uk
www.ahsoc.demon.co.uk

British Horological Institute (BHI)

The BHI is a professional horological body, about a third of its members are professional horologists. The BHI publishes a monthly magazine, has a library, good collection of turret clocks and runs a wide variety of training courses including turret clock restoration.

British Horological Institute
Upton Hall
Upton
Newark
Notts NG23 5TE
01636 813795
email clocks@bhi.co.uk
www.bhi.co.uk

Church Buildings Council (CBC)

The CBC is a constituent council of the General Synod of the Church of England and one of its duties is to advise Anglican churches on the care of the contents of churches. Specialist committees advise on monuments, stained glass, wall paintings, metal work, organs, bells and clocks. The Clocks Committee can award grants towards historic clock conservation. The CBC was formerly known as the Council for the Care of Churches (CCC) and before that the Council for the Places of Worship (CPW).

Church Buildings Council
Church House
Great Smith Street
London SW1P 3AZ
020 7898 1866
email ccb.enquiries@churchofengland.org
www.churchcare.co.uk

Bibliography

The following list of books are those which will give a new reader a good insight into turret clocks. Unfortunately many are out of print and may be difficult to obtain. Libraries which have a good collection of books on clocks are:—

Libraries
Antiquarian Horological Society Library
and
The Clockmakers' Company Library
(Both of the above are housed in the Guildhall Library, Aldermanbury, London EC2P 2EJ.)

The Science Museum Library, Exhibition Road, South Kensington, London. SW7 2DD

British Horlogical Institute (Members only)

Books on Turret Clocks
BEESON. C.F.C.
English Church Clocks 1280-1850.
Antiquarian Horological Society 1971
Brant Wright Associates 1977
The best modern book dedicated to turret clocks. An absolute must for the enthusiast even though it stops at 1850.

BEESON. C.F.C.
Perpignan 1356. The making of a clock and bell for the King's castle.
Antiquarian Horological Society 1971
The story of the making a medieval turret clock for the king in Perpignan in France.

BUNDOCK, Mike
Herne Bay Clock Tower
Pierhead Publications 2000
A history of an early purpose built clock tower.

BUNDOCK, Mike
Margate Clock Tower
Margate Civic Society 2013
A history of Margate's clock tower and time ball.

BUNDOCK Mike and McKAY. Chris
James W. Benson of Ludgate Hilll
Pierhead Publications 2002
Facsimile articles and catalogue of this firm of turret clock makers.

COUNCIL FOR THE CARE OF CHURCHES.
Turret Clocks. Guidelines for their Maintenance and Repair and for the Installation of Automatic Winders.
The booklet is aimed at parishes who need to have a basic understanding of the issues that involve clocks in their charge. Available for download from the CBC.
http://www.churchcare.co.uk/images/Churches_Guidance_Note_Turret_Clock.pdf

CRAVEN, Maxwell
The Smiths of Derby. A Journey Through Time.
Smith of Derby 2011
A history of Smiths of Derby told from the family history viewpoint.

DARWIN. John
The Triumphs of Big Ben.
R Hale London 1986
Easy to read history of Big Ben with particular reference to the 1976 failure. John Darwin was the Clerk of Works at the time of the 1976 disaster.

De CARLE. Donald.
British Time.
Crosby Lockwood, London 1959.
Quite a bit on Big Ben. Just right for those who don't want to go too deep.

DULEY. Anthony J.
The Medieval Clock of Salisbury Cathedral.
First printed in 1972 with many reprints.
A brief history of the clock's discovery, its "restoration", and a description of the movement.

FERRIDAY. Peter.
Lord Grimthorpe 1816-1905.
John Murray, London 1957.
A must for any Big Ben fan, or for those to whom Grimthorpe's crusty temperament appeals.

GORDON. G.F.C.
Clockmaking Past and Present.
Crosby Lockwood & Sons, London 1925. 1st Edition.
Trade Edition 1928. 229pp.
Technical Press Ltd, London 1949. 2nd enlarged edition.
This incorporates the more important portions of "Clocks Watches and Bells," by the late Lord Grimthorpe, relating to turret clocks and gravity escapements.

GRIMTHORPE. Edmund, Beckett, Lord. LL.D,.K.C., F.R.A.S.
A Rudimentary Treatise on Clocks and Watches, and Bells for Public Purposes. 404pp
Crosby Lockwood & Co London 1903. 8th Edition.

Facsimile reprint of 8th Edition 1974 by EP Publishing. The book was first publsihed in 1850 and went through 8 editions.
Downloadable for free from the internet from the Gutenberg Project
Also available as a print on demand facsimile book. Despite being last published in 1903 this book is an absolute must for turret clock students. Before being made a Peer, Lord Grimthorpe was first Edmund Beckett Denison, then Sir Edmund Beckett.

HELLYER, Brian & Heather
The Astronomical Clock at Hampton Court Palace .
HMSO 1973.
Description of clock and dial. Nice pictures of the 1947 restoration.

HEWITT, Pat.
Turret Clocks in Leicestershire and Rutland.
Leicestershire Museums and Arts & Record Services 1994.
A list of Leicestershire clock and makers.

HOUSES OF PARLIAMENT
Big Ben and the Elizabeth Tower
Houses of Parliament 2013
A booklet that is wonderful value and full of colour illustrations and a well informed history.

HOWGRAVE-GRAHAM, R.P.
The Wells Clock
Friends of Wells Cathdral 4th Edn 1978
A brief history of Wells Cathedral clock.

McDONALD, Peter
Big Ben: The Bell, the Clock and the Tower
Sutton Publishing 2004.
A general non-technical history of Big Ben. Has 14 illustrations.

McKAY. Chris.
Big Ben: The Great Clock and Bells at the Palace of Westminster'
Oxford University Press 2010.
A complete history of the clock tower, dials, clock and bells.

McKAY. Christopher (Editor)
The Great Salisbury Clock Trial
AHS 1993
Proceedings of a meeting organised by the Turret Clock Group; the Salisbury Cathedral clock was put on trial and accused of lying about its age.

McKAY. Chris.
Stands the Church Clock.
Bury St. Edmunds Leisure Services. 1989. A look behind the face of public timekeeping - history plus the catalogue of the 25 items which featured in the 1989 turret clock exhibition. 24pp.

McKAY. Chris. (Editor)
A Guide To Turret Clock Research.
Proceedings of a seminar organised by the Antiquarian Horological Society Turret Clock Group in 1991 to study research techniques. Ten papers cover subjects from looking at movements, through computers, to archives and Churchwardens' accounts. Of the ten four are case studies concerning a church clock, Herne Bay clock tower, a railway clock and clocks with an unusual pagoda-style frame. Overall, the emphasis of the book is on how to conduct research rather than on what was discovered.

McKAY. Chris
Smith & Son of Clerkenwell
Pierhead Publications 2001
Facsimile articles and catalogues of this firm of turret clock makers.

McKAY. Chris
John Moore & Sons of Clerkenwell. Turret Clock Makers
Pierhead Publications 2002
Facsimile articles of this firm of turret clock makers.

McKAY. Chris
James W. Benson of Ludgate Hill
Pierhead Publications 2001
Facsimile articles and catalogue of this firm of turret clock makers.

MERCER. Vaudrey.
Edward John Dent and his Successors.
Antiquarian Horological Society 1977.
A brilliant book on the Dent family that made turret clocks, good section on the Westminster Great Clock.

MERCER. Vaudrey.
A supplement to Edward John Dent and his Successors. (Published 1977)
Antiquarian Horological Society 1983.
5 pages on Big Ben, mentions the cause of the 1976 disaster. Has 4 folding plates in the back showing Denison's sketches for the Great Clock.

NETTELL. David.
An Amateur's Guide to Automatic Winders.
1988. 49pp. Soft cover.
Covers philosophy, types of winders, the Huygens endless chain, differential winders, monkey-up-the-rope winders, night silencing, safety, non-automatic winders, plus the practicalities of manufacturing auto winders.

NORTH, John
Richard of Wallingford.
Oxford University Press 1976.
A monumental three-volume set of the works of Abbot Richard of Wallingford who died in 1336. Richard designed a complex astronomical clock at St. Alban's Abbey. One volume has the Latin text and translation, the next diagrams and the third a commentary. Long out of print, expensive and an academic work.

NORTH, John
God's Clockmaker. Richard of Wallingford and the Invention of Time.
Richard of Wallingford
Continuum 2006
A history of Richard of Wallingford that is much more readable than the 1976 set.

PICKFORD. Chris (Editor)
Turret Clocks: Lists of Clocks from Makers' Catalogues and Publicity Materials.
Lists turret clock installations of famous and not so famous makers. Includes companies such as Smith, Potts, Gillett, Moore, Thwaites and Reed, and Vulliamy. AHS Turret Clock Group Monograph No 3 1995. Approx 190 pages, A4, Soft covers.
Second edition 2009 with additional information.
A treasure trove of information from turret makers.

POTTS, Michael.
Potts of Leeds. Five Generations of Clockmakers.
Mayfield Books 2006
A complete history of the Potts company. Well illustrated with lists of the clocks they produced.

REYNOLDS, Colin.
The Great George Liver Clock.
David Dover 2007.
A history of the design, manufacture and installation of the clocks on the Liver Building, Liverpool, by Gent of Leicester.

ROCK, Hugh
Church Clocks
Shire Publications 2008
A booklet showing lots of church clocks.

SHELLEY, Frederick
Early American Tower Clocks
NAWCC 1999.
Surviving American tower clocks from 1726 to 1870 with profiles of all known American makers. Over 250 illustrations.

THOMAS, Steve & Darlah.
Joyce of Whitchurch Clockmakers 1690-1965.
Inbeat Publications 2013.
A comprehensive history of the company with many colour plates.

UNGERER. Alfred
Les Horloges Astronomiques et Monumentales les plus remarquables
Published by the author 1931
In French. A 500 page survey of the world's turret clocks – a valuable reference work which is still of great interest.

VULLIAMY, Benjamin Lewis.
Some Considerations on the Subject of Public Clocks, Particularly Church Clocks.
1828.
Essentially the first specialist book in English on turret clocks. Long out of print but available on the net as a print on demand.

WILDING. John
A Modern Tower Clock Installation.
Meridian Clocks Sussex 1984 and Ritetime Publishing.
Reproduction of a series of constructional articles that commenced in the Horological Journal of 1984. The clock is electrical. A series aimed at the model engineer.

WILDING. John
A Small Weight Driven Tower Clock Movement.
Meridian Clocks Sussex and Ritetime Publishing.
Reproduction of a series of constructional articles that appeared in the Horological Journal. The clock is mechanical. A project for the model engineer.

WILDING. John
Notes on Tower Clocks their maintenance, repair and overhaul.
Ritetime Publishing 2005.
Reproduction of a series of articles that appeared in the Horological Journal. Various repairs are outlined to a clock that was restored. Only 3 pages are spent on maintenance. A note at the beginning states the book is for the home constructor only.

Basic Clock Care Guide Sheet

Safety

Check that all aspects of access to the clock are safe. Where ladders and platforms are involved, make sure ladders are secured and platforms have hand rails. If there are any problems report these to the person in charge. If working alone make sure someone knows where you are so they can check it you do not return.

Winding

If the clock has an maintaining power engage this before winding the going train. Wind carefully until the weight can be seen or a mark on the wire line is observed. Let the winding handle turn slowly backwards so that the click is lowered gently onto the ratchet. When winding an hour striking train do not wind this between when the clock has warned (about 5 minutes to the hour) and when the clock strikes. Similarly a quarter striking train should not be wound between 5 minutes to a quarter and the quarter.

Setting to time

Most clocks have an internal setting dial; often these run anti-clockwise. Use the key provided to turn the hands forward, do not use the hand on the setting dial. The hands can be turned backwards a small amount, but not past the hour or past the quarters in the case of a quarter striking clock. If the clock is an 18th century one where the pallets have to be disengaged to let the train run, then make sure the escape wheel arbor is held and allowed to turn only slowly otherwise damage is likely to be caused to the escape wheel teeth. To set the clock on an hour for summer time advance the hands pausing to allow the clock to complete striking on the quarters and hours. To put the clock back an hour for winter time it is probably best to stop the clock for an hour since striking clocks cannot be set backwards.

Regulating

If the clock loses slightly raise the pendulum bob by turning the rating nut. If it gains, lower the bob. To do this, first gently stop the pendulum by opposing its motion with your hand. A heavy pendulum must be dealt with gently to prevent damage to the suspension spring. This might be a two-man job, one to hold the pendulum to stop it twisting and the other to adjust the rating nut. To start the pendulum give gentle pushes to the pendulum until the clock starts to tick. One turn of the rating nut is likely to make a difference of a minute or more a day. Where a clock has regulating weights on the pendulum take weights off to make the clock lose and add weights to make the clock gain. This can be done with the pendulum swinging.

Correcting striking

If the hour or quarter striking has got out of step, lift the locking lever to allow the striking to run. Repeat until the correct quarter / hour has been sounded.

Do's & Don'ts

Do not oil a clock unless you know exactly what to do. Do not touch bells or bell ropes unless you are a ringer. Do carry on caring for the clock, the local community does appreciate it even though they probably never tell you.

Annual Maintenance

Have an annual maintenance contract for the clock. Its an excellent way of preserving the clock for the next generation.

From: The Turret Clock Keeper's Handbook by Chris McKay.

Rear Cover
Italian proverb
Warning sign to ringers to pull hammers off before ringing bell 1861

Printed in Great Britain
by Amazon